HANNAH WEST
in Deep Water

HANNAH WEST
in Deep Water

A Mystery by
Linda Johns

SLEUTH
PUFFIN

PUFFIN BOOKS

Published by the Penguin Group
Penguin Young Readers Group, 345 Hudson Street,
New York, New York 10014, U.S.A.
Penguin Group (Canada), 10 Alcorn Avenue,
Toronto, Ontario, Canada M4V 3B2
(a division of Pearson Penguin Canada Inc.)
Penguin Books Ltd, 80 Strand, London WC2R 0RL, England
Penguin Ireland, 25 St Stephen's Green, Dublin 2, Ireland
(a division of Penguin Books Ltd)
Penguin Group (Australia), 250 Camberwell Road, Camberwell,
Victoria 3124, Australia (a division of Pearson Australia Group Pty Ltd)
Penguin Books India Pvt Ltd, 11 Community Centre,
Panchsheel Park, New Delhi - 110 017, India
Penguin Group (NZ), Cnr Airborne and Rosedale Roads,
Albany, Auckland 1310, New Zealand (a division of Pearson New Zealand Ltd)
Penguin Books (South Africa) (Pty) Ltd, 24 Sturdee Avenue,
Rosebank, Johannesburg 2196, South Africa

Registered Offices: Penguin Books Ltd, 80 Strand,
London WC2R 0RL, England

This Sleuth edition first published by Puffin Books,
a division of Penguin Young Readers Group, 2006

1 3 5 7 9 10 8 6 4 2

Text copyright © Linda Johns, 2006
Illustrations copyright © Penny Carter, 2006

LIBRARY OF CONGRESS CATALOGING-IN-PUBLICATION DATA
Johns, Linda.
Hannah West in deep water: a mystery / by Linda Johns.
p. cm.
Summary: Pre-teen sleuth Hannah West investigates an environmental mystery while
staying in a houseboat on Seattle's Lake Washington.
ISBN 0-14-240700-3 (pbk.)
[1. Water—Pollution—Fiction. 2. Pollution—Fiction. 3. Television—Production and
direction—Fiction. 4. Washington, Lake (Wash.)—Fiction. 5. Seattle (Wash.)—Fiction
6. Mystery and detective stories.] I. Title.

PZ7.J6219Han 2006
[Fic]—dc22
2006044306

Printed in the United States of America

for Fred and Evvy Johns
—L. J.

CHAPTER 1

"I CAN'T BELIEVE YOU GET TO LIVE HERE," LILY SAID FROM THE BACKSEAT. "This is totally cool."

"Lucky for you that I still let you be my friend," I said. I was secretly pleased that Lily sounded impressed. Mom and I might be only temporary residents on Portage Bay, but you have to admit that it's a pretty sweet deal to get to live on a houseboat.

"There's the entrance to our dock," Mom said, pointing to a sidewalk that led toward Lake Washington. She pulled our battered old Honda Civic into a spot across the street. "It's a bit hidden from the street, but it's always easy to spot because of the mailboxes."

"Even our mailboxes are cool," I said smugly to Lily. I never gave much thought to mailboxes before except when I'd seen an occasional one shaped like Snoopy's dog house or with a propeller to look like an airplane or something. The Portage Bay dock mailboxes were the traditional metal style, but each had a fresh coat of paint in the solid, bright colors of blue, green, and white. Purple, red, and white flowers grew below the mailboxes, and even more bright blooms cascaded out of baskets positioned around the mailbox platform.

"It's just like *Sleepless in Seattle*," Lily said. "This is so exciting!"

It really was like *Sleepless in Seattle*, the 1990s movie with Tom Hanks and Meg Ryan. Much of the movie was set on a houseboat, giving the rest of the world the cockamamie idea that if you live in Seattle you could easily choose—and afford—to live on a houseboat. Actually, there are 570,000 people in Seattle and 1.8 million people in the county, but only five-hundred-some houseboats. That means only . . . well, you get the idea.

We stepped out of the car and into the rain. Now, I don't want you to get the wrong idea about Seattle. Despite its reputation as the Rainy City, Seattle is actually pretty sunny in the summer. Except for today, that is. Just figures that a nonstop drizzle fell from the sky to greet me on my first day as a houseboat resident. I was wearing long pants for the first time in two months.

"Maggie! There you are!" Rushing toward us came a gray-haired and bearded man pulling a rolling suitcase with one hand and holding an apricot-colored dog on a leash with the other.

"Hi, Jake. Are you leaving already?" Mom said.

"I'm so sorry. In the rush to get out of town I completely forgot to call and tell you that Heather wanted to get to the airport early. There's a new day spa there, and she needs a pedicure before we get on our flight," he said.

Lily and I rolled our eyes at each other. This guy was making it sound like a medical emergency when in fact his girlfriend just wanted to get her toenails painted before she went to France. He fumbled in his shoulder bag and jangled things around until he pulled out a set of keys and handed them to Mom. "I left a notebook of information on the desk for you and Hannah." He looked at Lily when he said my name. Lily doesn't look like blond, curly-haired Maggie West, but she's definitely a closer match to my mom than I am with my straight black hair, olive skin, and brown, almond-shaped eyes.

"That's me," I said, before Jake could embarrass himself by assuming that the Chinese girl couldn't be Maggie's daughter. "I'm Hannah, and this is my friend, Lily. And you must be Mango!" I bent down to meet Jake's apricot-colored dog.

3

"I'm going to miss Mango so much," Jake said, rather reluctantly handing the leash over to me. Jake looked seriously stressed about leaving his dog, which I fully expected based on the lengthy e-mail messages he'd sent Mom over the past few weeks. Jake wanted to be sure we knew all about labradoodles. That's right: labradoodles. You see, Mango is half Labrador retriever and half Standard poodle. But don't go thinking of him as a mutt, because these lab and poodle mixes are bred on purpose. In fact, it seemed as if labradoodles were the hot dogs of the year in Seattle. The poodle in them meant that they didn't shed, making them good for people with dog allergies. The Labrador in them assured that they'd be gentle, friendly, and loyal.

"Maggie, listen," Jake went on, "there's a film crew that's going to be here this week. I'm assured it's no big deal, but I thought I should warn you."

"Film crew? For a movie? Anyone famous going to be here?" Lily piped in. She's an actress impatiently waiting for her big break.

"What? Famous? Oh, the film. I don't know," Jake said distractedly. "It's a movie or something for a cable-TV channel."

I could tell that Lily was thinking "cable-TV

channel" could be the big time, especially if it was HBO or Showtime. I didn't want to point out that it could also be one of those public access channels, or maybe instead of a movie it was a program on saving salmon or the merits of proper dental hygiene.

A yellow cab pulled up to the curb and honked. A tall woman with high strappy sandals that made her even taller got out of the backseat and motioned impatiently toward us. Jake's face literally melted, going from stressed out to all soft and lovey-dovey when he saw her.

"There's Heather. I need to go." He hugged Mango again. "Thanks for everything, Maggie. Oh, one last thing." He pulled an envelope out of his bag and handed it to Mom. I was betting it was more instructions on caring for Mango. "I'm not sure how much the filming will disrupt things. But just in case it inconveniences you, here's a little something to make up for it."

"Thank you, but that's really not necessary," Mom began, but Jake was already rushing over to the cab. I snatched the envelope from Mom and took a quick look inside to find a restaurant gift certificate. Mom might be too polite to look inside in front of him, but it didn't matter anyway, because Jake had eyes only for

Heather. He gave her a quick kiss. I swear she rolled her eyes as he reached up and his lips made contact with her cheek. He was at least a half foot shorter than his girlfriend. I'm all for tall women and short men getting together with confidence, but this couple looked a bit cartoonish. Jake has that Mr. Northwest look—the kind of older guy who buys all his clothes at REI and hikes year-round and thinks it's acceptable to wear socks with hiking sandals. His girlfriend looked as if she'd send a servant outside to bend over to pick up the newspaper in the morning.

"We're going to be late," she snapped, moving away from him. "Just let the house sitters take care of everything." She said "house sitters" so that it sounded like "low-life servants."

"I'm so sorry. I'll make it up to you," Jake said, following her into the backseat of the taxi.

We watched as the taxi drove off, and then we headed toward the houseboat.

"Poor Jake. I hope they'll still be together after nine weeks in Europe," Mom said.

"I know what you mea—"

Splat! I slipped on the dock and fell flat on my butt. "Vincent! Pollock!" I cried, as the plastic bag I'd carried swooped out of my grasp.

Plop. It fell into the water.

Mango barked.

"No, Mango! No!" I cried.

And then . . . a much bigger *plop*.

CHAPTER 2

"MANGO, NO!" I CRIED, STRUGGLING TO GET UP. "IF HE BITES THAT plastic bag, it's all over for Vincent and Pollock," I whined as I watched him dog paddle toward the Ziploc bag that was serving as temporary transportation for my two goldfish.

"Here, Mango! Here, boy!" Mom joined me at the very edge of the dock, calling out to the dog, who was now in full fetch mode. He is, after all, half Labrador retriever. Then again, he's also half poodle, which might mean he'd decide to obey Mom's command and swim back to us.

Plop. Plop-plop.

A fluorescent green tennis ball landed in the water to the left of Mango's head. Two more tennis balls followed in quick succession.

"Get the ball, Mango," a small older woman instructed as she walked toward us. Obligingly, Mango turned his course toward the ball, intent on his mission.

"Good boy! Keep going!" Lily, Mom, and I cheered him on as if his task was the most difficult in the world. Mango glided through the water, bringing the tennis ball back to the edge of the dock. The woman bent over to get it from him and to scratch him behind the ears. "Good boy! Now get the other ones! Get them!" she commanded.

"I didn't really need to tell him to get the other balls. He's obsessed with tennis balls, and he won't stop until he gets them all," she told us. "Here, you can toss this one again if he gets the other two before I get back." She handed me the soggy green ball and headed into a white houseboat with green trim. She came back out with a net and a paddle. "Keep telling him he's a good boy. I'll get your package. What's in it, by the way?" She kept talking while she effortlessly lifted a kayak off the dock, lowered it into the water, and then slipped inside and pushed herself off from the dock.

"My goldfish. They're in a plastic bag," I said, pointing. "Do you see them? It kind of looks like a bubble. Oh, good dog, Mango." I accepted the third soggy tennis ball from him and then hurled it out farther into the water, just to make sure he'd stay occupied until Vincent and Pollock got safely back.

"Got it!" the woman called from the kayak. "Or should I say, 'got them'? Because it looks like there are two perfectly fine goldfish inside here."

"Thank you so much!" I was practically shrieking with happiness. When you're technically homeless like Mom and me, you get pretty attached to the few things that you have. And I'm terribly attached to my two goldfish named after Vincent van Gogh and Jackson Pollock, two of my all-time-favorite artists. My fish rescuer pulled her kayak up to the dock and handed my pets to me. I kissed the plastic bag, wishing once again that they were the kind of pets you could pet and nuzzle. Right then Mango, a big bundle in need of some grateful nuzzling, returned to the dock, too.

"Lily, will you hold my boys?" I handed the fish to her so I could bend down and get the ball from Mango. I clumsily helped him get back up on the dock, a chore that left me almost as wet as the shaggy, soaked dog. He tried to lick the water off me, which made me laugh so hard that he easily knocked me over. While I was being a total dog-loving klutz, the woman had somehow gotten herself and her kayak out of the water without so much as a drop of water getting on her.

"Thank you so much for your help," Mom said to the

woman. "I'm afraid we made a bit bigger splash than I'd hoped for when we arrived."

"Don't worry about it," the mystery woman said. "Mango was just doing his job. It's what he was bred to do. Or at least, it's what half of him was bred to do. Jake gave me those tennis balls when I was dog-sitting Mango."

"They certainly came in handy today," I said. "I really want to thank you for saving Vincent and Pollock."

"Vincent and Pollock? What great names. Makes me think of two of my favorite artists," she said. "Are you by chance an art lover?"

"I am," I said.

"It's not often that I meet a teenager who likes my two favorite artists," she said.

I didn't say anything because I was busy thinking how much I liked being called a teenager, which I'm not. Not yet. I'm still twelve.

"She's an artist, too," Lily piped in. "I'm her agent."

"And I'm her mother," Mom said. "Alice, I'd like you to meet my daughter, Hannah West, and her friend, Lily Shannon. Girls, this is Alice Campbell. Jake introduced me to her the first time I came to see him. He said that anything we want to know, we can just ask Alice."

Alice smiled and held her hand out to shake. Her eyes twinkled as she looked directly at me. She looked Japanese, but I wasn't sure. There wasn't any clue in her name. Then again, there isn't any real clue in my name that I'm Chinese, unless you associate my middle name, Jade, with China (which is exactly why it's my middle name).

"I'm also a dog walker," I said.

I handed her my card, which unfortunately was a little soggy:

HANNAH J. WEST
PET SITTER, DOG WALKER, PLANT WATERER
AND ALL AROUND ERRAND GIRL
235-6628

"Delightful! Nice to meet you, too, Lily," she said, shaking Lily's hand.

I liked Alice Campbell immediately. Not only had she saved my fish, but she wasn't treating us like little kids.

"Welcome to the Portage Bay Floating Home Association," Alice said. "Maggie, I'm betting that what Jake really said is that I'm president of our little association here. Please don't hesitate to ask if you need anything. You'll find that everyone on this particular dock is extremely friendly. We all look out for one another. Your next-door neighbors, Mike and Betsy, are on vacation right now. And so is Patrick down on this end. But everyone else is around and excited to meet you. I'd love to invite you in for tea, but I'm sure you want to get settled."

"Hannah hasn't even seen the inside of the houseboat yet," Mom said.

"You'll love it, I'm sure. Now, I hate to be bossy," Alice continued in a tone of voice that people use when they say that they hate to be bossy, but then they act bossy anyway. "But before you leave, you need to bring Mango over to my porch so we can rinse him off. In fact, we'll give him a full bath. Now, now, now. I insist." I could tell there was no getting Mango out of this bath.

"Didn't he just have a bath in the lake?" Lily asked.

"No!" Alice said sharply. "He must be thoroughly cleaned if he gets lake water on him. Jake may have neglected to tell you that, but I assure you, it's terribly important. Hannah, please promise me that you'll clean Mango thoroughly if he gets any lake water on him."

"Um, okay," I said, a bit confused about the sudden urgency in her voice.

"In fact, I encourage you to take a shower since he

shook water all over you, too," she said. I gave her a look that must have conveyed what was going through my head: Are you crazy? It's just a little bit of water. She seemed to read my mind.

"Well, at least you should all wash your hands. Now, let's get this dog hosed off," she said. There didn't seem to be any question that Mango was getting a full dock-side scrub down, complete with some lavender-scented Buddy Wash dog soap.

"Do you have a dog?" I asked Alice.

"Oh, no," she said, still intently scrubbing and rinsing Mango.

"I was just wondering why you have dog soap handy," I said.

"Sometimes I give Mango a bath. Jake's good about rinsing him off after muddy walks or when he gets in the water here, but I think he needs a little more."

It seemed a little presumptuous for someone to give someone else's dog a bath, but I was new here. Maybe it was the kind of place where bathing a dog is like baking brownies to show your neighbors you like them. Or maybe Alice was an obsessive clean freak and people happily left the pet bathing in her capable hands. It was curious but didn't really matter. I just wanted to get this dog clean and toweled off so I could see our new house.

Okay, okay. It's not really "our" house. And I'm not really homeless, either. Although technically I don't have a permanent address. Don't get all panicky like we're cagey criminals or in the witness protection program or something. We're professional house sitters, which sounds glamorous, but it means that we pack up and move every couple of weeks. This was our first time house-sitting in a houseboat, or a "floating home" as those in the know say. It was going to feel more like being on vacation than house-sitting. It was an extra bonus that the house came with a dog. I've done tons of dog walking before, but never round-the-clock doggy duty.

After two rounds of sudsing and three rinses, Alice deemed Mango clean and ready to go. Finally! "Let's go home, boy," I said, and Lily, Mom, and I followed Mango down the dock. I'd been so busy worrying about Vincent, Pollock, and Mango that I hadn't really looked at the houseboats on our L-shaped dock. Each house was painted a fresh, warm color—vibrant blue, true red, a deep gray that somehow looked cheery—or a bright white. Windows and trim were painted a distinctly contrasting color, giving each little house a crisp, clean look. Window boxes and terra-cotta planters over- flowed with flowers blooming in reds, purples, blues, hot pinks, and whites. I felt as if I was in a poster-sized print of a charming alley in a European village. Everything was fresh and gorgeous, complemented by the gentle lapping sound of the water under the dock. Mom had told me that Jake's cottage had the best spot on the dock, since it was at the very end of the "L" with water surrounding it on three sides. The house was blue with white-and-purple trim.

A rustling noise caught my attention just before I got to our entrance. I turned to look. Two people dressed head to toe in black rain gear scurried out from the cottage porch next door. Each black-hooded figure carried two large white buckets as they practically trotted back toward the street. Weird. Alice Campbell had just told us that our next-door neighbors were on vacation. Maybe people rich enough for houseboats get their houses cleaned even when they're not there.

"Welcome home!" Mom said as she opened the deep purple door of our houseboat. Her arms stretched wide. "Come inside and check it out!"

Mango obviously didn't need an invitation. He barreled past Mom and up the first two rungs of a ladder-style staircase that went up to a sleeping loft above. I heard a cat meow from the loft area. "That must be Hank," I said. Hank was Jake's cat. I'd already heard that Mango loved Hank, but the cat was not returning the sentiment.

"This is fabulous!" Lily gushed. I walked into a small kitchen that opened up to a light-filled living room with wall-to-wall windows. A deck wrapped around the north and east sides of the living room, making it seem as if the whole house was floating on Lake Washington. Wait. What am I saying? The whole house *was* floating on Lake Washington. It was so quiet this morning that I could hear the water lapping gently under the dock. I felt surrounded by water, but not wobbly like I would be if I were on a raft or in a boat. I explored every inch of the cottage, which didn't take long. The house was teensy tiny, but each room was perfect. My bedroom, which was really a guest room and office, had two windows facing toward the street, but with lots of water between me and the street. Bright red gera-niums, purple petunias, and cascading vines with little white flowers spilled out of the window boxes. I could crank open the windows and smell the fresh lake water below. Bookshelves and wood file cabinets lined the walls. A twin bed was shoved under a window, seeming more like a couch than a bed. But there was a laptop on the built-in desk and a small flat-screen TV on top of a dresser. Seemed like an ideal bedroom to me.

I followed Mom's voice up a ladder to the loft bedroom, which she obviously claimed as her own. She was the adult, after all. There was a big bed with a fluffy white down comforter and a half-dozen pillows piled on top. The room was open to the living room and windows below. It reminded me of a crow's nest on a big sailing ship.

Mango whined from down below. The ladder was too steep for him, a fact that obviously didn't escape the agile cat. Hank taunted him from above.

"It's okay, boy," I said, climbing back down. "Where do you sleep? Can you show me your bed?"

His ears perked up when I said "bed."

"Go to bed?" I asked hesitantly.

Mango trotted off to my bedroom and jumped up on the bed. He looked so proud of himself. "Good boy," I said, giving him a scratch behind the ears. "I think I have a bunk mate," I called up to Mom.

"Judging by all the cat hair, I think Hank likes to bunk up here," Mom said. "Jake said he left information in your room to let you know all you need for Mango. Have you come across it yet?"

I scanned the desk, looking for a note about dog care. Instead I found a two-inch-wide purple three-ring binder with a carefully made spine label that read MANGO CARE AND OTHER IMPORTANT INFORMATION. I pulled it out. The front of the notebook had a large color photograph of Mango, with the same words printed over the photo. Inside was a table of contents and carefully labeled sections that included "Feeding Mango," "Approved Training for Mango," and "Suggested Walking Routes for Mango." There were sections devoted to Mango's coat, teeth, and eyes, as well as emergency information about his veterinarian. The last section included general information about labradoodles, most of which he'd already e-mailed to us. An article on crossbreeding talked about other hot poodle mixes. It seems lots of people were intrigued with the idea of getting nonshedding dogs. Mix a cocker spaniel with a poodle and you get a cockapoo; take a miniature schnauzer and a poodle and you have a schnoodle; add a golden retriever to a poodle for a goldendoodle. The shih tzu and poodle mix had a couple of pretty funny combinations, too.

I looked at Mango. He looked like a regular, sweet dog to me. And right now he was looking at me as if I could be his favorite person in the world, if only I'd get on top of the bed with him and snuggle for a little while. "Later, boy," I said, giving him a big bear hug. He rewarded me with a moan of happiness.

"This is totally *Sleepless in Seattle*," Lily said from the living room. I headed back to the waterside room. I looked outside and saw a motorboat slowly pass by and then pick up speed. A sailboat with its mast down and its motor on puttered slowly past. I pulled out the camera my photography teacher had lent me and took a few shots. A few more boats passed by. One stopped, and I used the telephoto lens to zoom in. Two people wearing black rain gear were fiddling with something in the back. The taller one raised a white five-gallon bucket upside down over the side of the boat. The way he was flinging it around made it seem as if it was empty, sort of how those two people on the dock had been swinging empty white buckets. Those two people on the dock had also been wearing black. Hmmm . . . I zoomed in as much as I could, but it didn't do me much good because they weren't facing me. I clicked anyway. Darn! I was at the end of a twenty-four-exposure roll of film and I'd wasted at least six shots on those bucket people. The engine on the boat started up again, and they motored off. I sighed and rewound my film.

I loved this 35-millimeter manual Konica camera. It belonged to Greg, my photography teacher at Coyote Central, this cool middle school arts camp where I had a scholarship. I'd just finished a three-week photography class at Coyote, and he had let me experiment with a couple of his cameras. Until then I'd used only disposable or digital cameras, or those kind that auto-focus, auto-advance, and auto-everything. Photography was so much more fun with a camera that allows you to experiment with the focus and the aperture (which controls the amount of light that comes through). In drawing, sometimes I have to stop and let my eyes relax so I can see things fresh. I was finding that the same thing helped in photography, because otherwise it's too easy to get obsessed with looking at life through a lens. I closed my eyes and opened them to see if anything new appeared.

Nope. Just a bunch of boats. But soon a bit of a pattern emerged. Sailboats seemed to be heading one way; motorboats, the opposite direction.

"I'm guessing that the sailboats are heading out to the Puget Sound," Mom said, as she walked into the room and saw me looking at the boat traffic. "Remember how Robert used to rave about that?" There's a ship canal that links Lake Washington—where

21

we were living—with Lake Union and the Puget Sound. It meant that boaters had the best of fresh water and salt water accessible to them. It didn't mean much to me, but grown-ups around here get all excited about the waterways. Robert, one of Mom's old bosses at MegaComp, used to go on and on about how "fabulous" it is to get in a boat on the far shore of Lake Washington in the morning and be up at an island in the Puget Sound in the afternoon.

"It was all he ever talked about," I added.

"Well, some people take their boating pretty seriously," she said. "And from what I hear, the motorboaters are even more into it than the sailboaters."

I let my mind wander to the idea that I was now living in the midst of all these serious boaters. And even if we weren't going to be out there cruising with them, I was feeling pretty happy about the prospect of waking up on Lake Washington in the morning and going to sleep on Lake Washington at night. And I do mean *on* the lake.

CHAPTER 3

"WHOA! MY LEGS FEEL ALL WOBBLY AND WEIRD!" I SAID WHEN I GOT back on solid land. I'd been on the houseboat for three hours and I already had my sea legs, I guess, because on land my legs felt like rubber. It took only a couple of steps before I was back to normal, though.

"Jake told me that it might feel weird to us for the first few seconds on land each day," Mom said. She and I were taking Mango on a walk around the Portage Bay neighborhood. Lily's parents had already picked her up, with a promise that she'd come back many, many times while we were living on the water. If word got out about where we were living, I could become quite popular, I bet. But, as always, we kept our house-sitting adventures hush-hush, particularly from the Seattle school district. Without a north Seattle address, I wouldn't be able to keep going to Cesar Chavez Middle School with Lily.

As we continued on our walk, Mom started pointing out street names. Ever since I was little, Mom had this annoying habit of reading street signs and addresses to me. It drove me crazy—and it still drives me crazy—but it has made it easier for me to find my way around. At a very early age, I learned that avenues ran north-south in Seattle and that streets ran east-west. It was pretty easy to figure out because the streets were set up like grids. Except in this neighborhood.

"None of the streets are straight! This is so confusing," I grumbled.

"Some of the streets follow the shoreline, but you'll get the hang pretty quickly," she said, pointing out that we were walking on Boyer Avenue. "This is the most important street for you to remember because—"

"Doughnuts straight ahead!" I cried.

"I was going to say because there's a bus stop in front of the Canal Market, but if it helps you get oriented by knowing they have doughnuts, then so be it," Mom said.

Mango was obviously a regular at the Canal Market. He knew just where to sit and wait while we went in to check out the doughnuts. He also seemed to know that no one exits the store without getting a dog treat. We left, and as we ate our doughnuts, we walked about nine blocks farther to a busy corner I recognized because of a Red Robin restaurant on the right. Our street intersected with Eastlake Avenue East, a street I knew well from the number 66.

"You're checking out the bus stops, aren't you?" Mom said.

"Yep."

"And I'm guessing that you've already memorized the routes and times by looking at the Metro schedule online?" she asked.

"Yep again. Except it's way better to actually see the bus stop than to just look on a map, especially when curvy streets are involved," I said. I was so relieved to see that I could walk straight down our street about twelve blocks to get on my favorite bus. Then it was just a couple miles south to get downtown or about five miles north to get to my old Maple Leaf neighborhood, where Lily still lived.

"We'll have to check out the number 25, too," Mom said.

"It comes every eighteen to twenty minutes during peak times, beginning at approximately six twenty-two A.M. To head downtown, I board on our side of the street, arriving downtown approximately thirteen minutes later. If I board on the other side of the street,

I can get to the University of Washington, go shopping at University Village, or go to some neighborhood called Laurelhurst at any time after six thirty-one A.M.," I rattled off.

"Good to know," Mom said, looking suitably impressed.

"But be forewarned that midday the number 25 comes only once an hour," I said.

"You'll have to plan ahead," Mom said. "Or take another bus." She wrapped an arm around my shoulders, which I knew was her cornball-Mom way of saying that she was proud of my independence. At least that's what I choose to think it meant. We walked back on the opposite side of the street, passing our dock and continuing on past the sprawling St. Demetrios Greek Orthodox Church. Street after street of brick houses with pointy roofs and immaculate gardens welcomed us as we meandered past the Emerald City Yacht Club and the Montlake Community Center, where I first learned to play ultimate Frisbee, and into the arboretum. I've been to the Washington Park Arboretum (its official name) dozens of times on school field trips or with out-of-town relatives, but I'd never lived so close. I couldn't believe we could walk to so many things.

By the time we got back to our houseboat more than an hour later, the sun was out in full force. Mom and I decided to go out on the lake. Mango watched us from the living room window as we pushed off in Jake's double kayak.

"This is the life!" I said from the front seat. "We just walk out our door, put our boat in the water, and start paddling."

"I could definitely get used to this," Mom said.

We headed around the corner to Lake Union. We'd passed several other houseboat docks, but there was a certain houseboat Mom was determined we see.

I had a feeling she was taking me to see the houseboat from *Sleepless in Seattle*, a movie we'd watched about eleven times already. I'd also gone past the boat on a tour with Grandma earlier in the summer.

Mom pulled her paddle hard on the starboard side for the next two strokes so that we took a sharp turn to the left. "Let's hug the shore on this side," she said. "As you can see, we're on the opposite side of the lake from the *Sleepless* house, in case you were worried I was going to make you go by it. There are some other things I want to show you." She'd recently read a book about floating homes in Seattle and was hot to show off her new knowledge. Mom was always reading all these random books and articles, which, she said, made her an expert on absolutely nothing but a darn good Trivial Pursuit and Jeopardy player. Her arsenal of knowledge (or random facts) could sometimes be interesting, when it wasn't annoying. This time it was pretty interesting, as she pointed out a houseboat that actually had a basement with a fitness center and a wine cellar. As I struggled to wrap my head around the idea of a houseboat with a basement, we went by small, tidy floating homes that looked similar to the ones on our Portage Bay dock. We also went by some floating homes that were more like floating mansions, kind of like the huge beige houses you see out in the suburbs. Mom and her friend Mary Perez call them McMansions. It seemed odd and out of scale to see a McMansion next to a tiny wood cottage.

"I feel like we're a million miles away from our real life," I said to Mom. "Almost like we're in a different country or something."

"That, my dear daughter, is exactly where we're about to be."

"Does that mean you're going to make me keep paddling until we get to Canada? Yikes! Hey, what's that?" I'd just spied a houseboat with colorful art and sculptures surrounding it. A flag with a white background flew at full mast from a large pole. The upper left corner of the flag had diagonal yellow and orange stripes; floating off center in the white area were some light blue stripes. The flag, the house, and the dock looked so colorful and chaotic compared to the tidy houses at the neighboring docks. I loved it immediately.

"That's the Archipelago of Tui Tui," Mom said excitedly.

"Huh?" My mind was combing back over the vocabulary lists and geography lessons from sixth grade. Archipelago, archipelago. Right! *Archipelago: A group of islands in a large body of water.*

But that didn't make any sense.

"Where's the island?" I asked.

"The house itself is an island nation," Mom said. "The owner seceded from the United States. He even has his own currency and postage stamps." As if on cue, when Mom said "owner," a man walked out on the dock and waved to us. At least I thought he was waving to us. I waved back, but then he seemed to be glaring at us, as if he'd just noticed us.

"You're making this all up, aren't you?" I asked.

"Good afternoon, neighbors!" I looked behind us and saw another kayak coming up quickly. It was

Alice Campbell. "Small world, isn't it? I'm just on my way to Tui Tui. I'll be back in the United States soon enough." She pulled up alongside the island nation of Tui Tui and put a soft-side Polar Bear thermal bag on the dock. It was one of those coolers that holds only about a six-pack of soda. She was talking to the man on the dock, who was gesturing and pointing out in the water. Who was he? The king of Tui Tui? The prime minister? Or just Mr. Tui Tui? And how did a houseboat in the middle of Seattle become an independent state? I still couldn't believe this was true, and I intended to do some research as soon as I got back to my laptop.

Mr. Tui Tui held up a glass jar filled with liquid and showed it to Alice before putting it in the cooler. He put two more jars in the cooler, which she then stowed in her kayak's cargo area. He helped her push off from the dock and waved her on her way.

I watched as Alice paddled east toward Portage Bay. Mom steered us over to Aqua Verde Café, the restaurant that Jake had given us the gift certificate for. We could pull right up in our kayak, and the dockhand would help us out and pull our boat out—sort of like valet parking for kayaks. It's my absolute favorite restaurant in Seattle, and even though I've been kayaking since I was in kindergarten, it was the first time I'd pulled up in my own boat. Yeah, I know, it's not really my kayak. But I was feeling pretty richie-rich right about then.

CHAPTER 4

I WOKE UP THE NEXT MORNING TO SOME OBNOXIOUS KNOCKING. I WAITED for Mom to answer, but she must have been in the bathroom getting ready to go to work.

"Hello! Anyone in there?" A voice now accompanied the knocking. Mango answered the question with a series of barks.

"Oh great. Just my luck. No one's home but they left a dog in here. Joshua is going to go ballistic about this," a woman's voice muttered. She started rapping on the door again, a little more aggressively, as if her noise would make someone—other than a barking dog—appear.

Mom doesn't like me to answer the door when she's in the shower, but this knocking and barking had to stop. "Mango! Quiet! Good boy," I cooed. "Who's there on the other side of the door? Because there's about a dozen of us on this side."

"A dozen? Just my luck that there'd be twelve people in the way," the voice on the other side whined. "Wait. You're kidding, right?"

I didn't reply. Let her sweat it out, with me and my eleven friends on the Extreme Quiet Team. "Listen, I'm with the film crew, and we've got to make sure that everyone's out before we start filming today. Didn't they leave you a production schedule?"

"No, I don't have a production schedule," I said, trying to sound like an annoyed adult executive. "Let me check with my mom." That last comment kind of blew my cover.

I stuck my head into the bathroom and asked my mom if she had any idea what was going on.

"I completely forgot about the filming schedule," she said. "I'm so sorry. I shouldn't have said I'd work this morning. Let's see if Lily's family can come get you."

"I can take care of myself," I said. "I'm used to spending time alone."

"I know, I know. But this is different. You won't have anywhere to go."

I could see her point. I didn't much like the idea of Mango and me hanging out on a park bench all day.

I went back to the woman who was waiting at the door. "Can't I just stay inside if we don't make any noise? I won't be any trouble," I tried one last time, trying to stand tall and look older.

"Sorry, but no," said the young woman with the clipboard. "You don't look like the troublemaking type. It's just that Joshua, the continuity guy, will have a total freak-out if any little thing changes from scene to scene."

"Okay, I'll leave, but it's my opinion that an occasional background noise, such as a dog bark, could add a little authenticity to your show." I started pulling my sandals on and tossing keys, dog treats, poop bags, a water bottle, my camera, and my cell phone into my messenger bag.

"I agree completely. But my boss won't. I'm just the P.A.," she said.

I looked at her blankly.

"Production assistant. I'm just the production assistant. My name is Celeste, by the way. This is only my second P.A. gig. But I learned the hard way earlier this year that even if you think everything is the same, Joshua can spot the teensiest detail changing from shot to shot. You could open a window a crack, or change the blinds. And then I'll hear about it. Like that leaf." She was off whisking a leaf off the dock. I watched her with fascination, until something else caught my eye.

An older woman dressed in a black nylon tracksuit peered around the corner of the cottage next to ours. Mom had confirmed last night that no one was home next door to us. It might make sense that house cleaners were there yesterday, but why would someone be back so soon? Or so early in the day? Our eyes met briefly, and then she backed around the corner again. I was tempted to say, "Hey, Celeste, what about that woman? How come you aren't on her case to leave?" But someone else was demanding the production assistant's attention.

"Celeste! We're ready to set up. Everything ready on your end?"

"Just about," Celeste said. She turned toward me, adding, "I need this place cleared out in ten minutes, okay?" While Celeste's back was turned, the woman in black did a modified speedwalk down the dock and toward the street. She carried two large white buckets, one in each hand. They must have been empty, because those things were almost two feet tall and they didn't seem to slow her down.

I closed the door and gave Mom the update. In the few minutes that I had spent talking to Celeste, she had already managed to get in touch with Lily's dad—who was going to come pick up Mango and me—and was nearly ready to leave for work. Within five minutes, she and I were headed toward the street.

It was like a different world had sprung up while we slept. Large white umbrellas and light boxes were set up along the dock. Three huge white trucks and trailers, the kind without any logos or names, were taking up most of the street. A police officer was directing cars to turn off Boyer and onto side streets. Any doubts I'd had about whether they were really making a legitimate TV show here vanished. These trucks were the real thing. Seattle isn't exactly New York or L.A., but the city gets a surprising amount of movie, TV, and commercial action. I've spent enough time downtown to know that those seemingly nondescript cargo trucks and vans carry lights, metal rigging, cameras, and tons of other equipment. Even the food wagon is usually unmarked. It's like they're trying to go all incognito by not drawing attention to themselves, but the mere fact that a series of these vehicles are parked on a street is like a beacon proclaiming, "Hollywood has come to your little town." It makes me think of a movie star wearing dark sunglasses—inside.

"Hannah! Over here!" Lily called to me. She and her dad were just getting out of their Subaru.

"Wow, I can't believe you made it down here already" I said to Dan, Lily's dad.

"Well, as soon as Lily heard the words 'film' and 'crew,' there was no way she was going to miss out on the action," Dan said. "She practically pushed me out the door as soon as I got off the phone."

"Let's go see who's here," Lily said, smoothing some watermelon-flavored balm on her lips. We headed back to the dock, leaving my mom and Dan to figure out the game plan for the rest of the day.

"You're hoping to get picked up as an extra, aren't you?" I asked.

"Aren't *you?*" Lily, the aspiring actress, asked, cocking her right eyebrow. "Check this out! I finally perfected the one-eyebrow-up-at-a-time look! Anyway, we can make some money and get discovered. It will probably just be the first of many film roles for me, but at least you'll get a little spending money and the joy of seeing your name in credits this one time."

"Thanks for all the confidence you have in me," I said. Lily blew me a kiss and put on her sunglasses.

"Look out!" said a bearded guy balancing a six-foot metal contraption on top of his shoulder. He'd just missed a woman in black rain gear who had come off the dock, and then the beam swung toward us. Lily and

I jumped to the side. The woman must have had a part in the movie, which would explain why she was wearing a waterproof get up—in black, no less—on a sunny Seattle day.

"So, who's in this movie anyway?" Lily asked.

"I have no idea," I said. "I don't even know what they're—"

"Aaaaarrrrgggghhhh!" A high-pitched scream interrupted me mid-sentence. Then a splash and . . .

Another scream. This time louder and shriller, coming from out by the dock where the film crew was.

Maybe it was part of the TV show, but it's true what they say about heart-stopping, bloodcurdling screams. My heart felt all panicky, and my blood felt weird. That's some good acting going on.

Only it turns out it wasn't acting.

"They're dead!" a woman screamed. "They're all dead!"

CHAPTER 5

MANGO YANKED HIS LEASH AND STARTED RUNNING TOWARD THE DOCK. I went along, as if I had any choice when a seventy-five-pound dog with the strength of a two-hundred-pound adult was pulling me. Then again, it's not as if I wasn't willing. Something big was happening.

"What if we get down there and find out it was part of the script?" Lily said, running alongside Mango and me.

I slowed down a tiny bit and pulled the pooch back, too. "That would be kind of embarrassing," I admitted.

"You can't just run toward danger, Hannah," Lily said. "We could ruin the shot."

That slowed me down even more. "Shot? We could get shot?"

"No! We could *ruin* the shot. As in, get in the way of the camera."

"That definitely could be kind of embarrassing," I said.

"It's not just kind of embarrassing. It's completely and unforgivingly embarrassing," Lily said.

A bout of embarrassment wasn't going to stop Mango and me, however. I have a nose for crime, and I could smell something going on. Well, I couldn't actually *smell* anything going on, although some sort of aroma had definitely piqued Mango's interest. There was a lot of commotion and splashing at the end of the dock.

"Let's just check it out," I said to Lily. "No one will notice us."

"I can't work in these conditions," a weepy and extremely wet woman said as two men helped pull her out of Lake Washington. Another woman immediately draped a blanket around the shivering actress. "The original script I approved didn't have a water shot," she said. Her teeth chattered, but her voice projected loud and clear. "I agreed to be a good sport today and go along with your changes, Marcus. But there are dead fish in the water! I think I touched them."

Dead fish? I looked over the edge of the dock where we stood, expecting to see some foot-long salmon belly up or something. But I couldn't see anything except dark water. I tightened my grip on Mango's leash.

"Who is that?" I whispered to Lily. I expect her to

know the names of famous people since her mom gets *People* magazine, but Lily just shrugged. She was intently taking in the film scene.

The wet actress was chewing out a man with a base-ball cap and black-framed sunglasses. "You're going to have to call a wrap for today, Marcus. I absolutely cannot work in these conditions. You'll need to rewrite this scene for me," she said, shrugging off a second blanket that some woman was trying to drape around her. "And I expect to have my shoes replaced by the time I get to the hotel." One of the crew members had just pulled a high-heeled green-and-gold sandal out of the water. He started to hand it to her, but she turned away from him. "Not that one! I want new shoes," she screeched. "Cynthia! Call the salon at Gene Juarez. Tell them it's an emergency and they need to get me in for a full Dead Sea salt scrub and wrap. I'll definitely need a hot stone massage as well."

"Yes, Miss Heathcliff," replied a young woman with a clipboard and a cell phone.

"Monica, please," the baseball cap man said. "It's just a little lake water. Think of it as getting back to nature."

"Marcus, I assure you, dead fish are not part of nature." The actress narrowed her eyes and scowled at the man she'd called Marcus. She tossed aside the blanket she'd been given and teetered toward the street in a left-right and up-down motion, since she had on only one high-heeled shoe.

"Monica," he called after her. "You're absolutely right to take the rest of the day off. Get some rest. We'll talk tonight."

"So that's Monica Heathcliff," Lily said to me. "I didn't recognize her soaking wet." The name didn't mean anything to me, and so far I wasn't too impressed with this actress's people skills.

"Okay, everyone, let's take a break. Be back here in forty-five. We'll need to get some more shots with this same lighting."

They were breaking after about fifteen minutes of working? Maybe I could get interested in this Hollywood scene.

"Hey, girls, what are you doing out here?" Mom rushed up behind us.

"That's exactly what I want to know," the guy named Marcus said, glaring at us. "What are you doing on my set?"

Mom immediately held out her hand and said, "I'm Maggie West, the house sitter for one of the residents on the dock."

"Marcus Dartmouth, director, *Dockside Blues*," he

42

said, in that fast-clipped way people who think they're important always introduce themselves on TV shows.

"Nice to meet you," Mom said. "The girls were just—"

But Marcus Dartmouth, director, interrupted her. "The house sitter? The sister, right? What a cushy gig. Excuse me!" He abruptly turned away and started barking out commands to a guy and a girl schlepping around lights and big white umbrellas.

"Whose sister are you?" Lily asked.

"I have absolutely no idea who or what he's talking about," Mom said. She didn't exactly answer Lily, but that's because Lily knows everyone in our family and was well aware of the fact that Mom was an only child. Just like me.

"Maybe he thinks you look like Monica Heathcliff when she's dry," I said.

"I'm sure he thinks that my frizzed-out curly hair and the dark circles under my eyes make me look just like a movie star," Mom said sarcastically.

"Excuse me, but you need to clear the dock." It was Celeste, the P.A.

"Right, we were just—" Mom started to say.

"Now, actually. You need to clear it now."

What's with these Hollywoodesque folks? They never seem to let Mom finish a sentence. Celeste was full of bravado, but she looked more nervous than before. A short man in a fedora stood about twenty feet down the dock watching her. He flipped open a cell phone and punched in a couple of numbers. Celeste's phone rang, and she answered immediately.

"Get rid of them," the man down the dock said into the phone. This must be the notorious Joshua.

Hello! Standing close enough to hear you, mister. I couldn't help but stare at him.

"Right away," Celeste said. They flipped their phones shut at the same time.

"Sorry, we're just leaving," I said, hoping her boss would be impressed with her for getting us set-crashers out of the way.

"Let's go," Mom said. She sounded impatient, with a tone that doesn't often creep into her voice.

Mom and Lily were already halfway toward the street, but I was purposely lagging behind. Mango wasn't that excited to leave familiar territory, which turned out to be helpful cover for me as I watched the woman in the black tracksuit—the one whom I had spotted while I was talking to Celeste. She was crouching low on the dock, scooping water by the spot where Monica Heathcliff had fallen into the water. I was pretty sure it wasn't the same woman I had seen in the black rain gear.

Maybe this was part of the TV crew, too, but she didn't seem like the Hollywood type. Then again, maybe she had some sort of behind-the-scenes job. From what I could tell so far, there was one actress and about thirty other people working hard to make her look good. Maybe this woman was part of the continuity team and her job was to make sure that every molecule of water looked the same from scene to scene.

Mango barked a short, friendly yip, and the woman turned.

It was Alice.

I knew she saw us, but she didn't wave. Or even smile. She turned back to the water.

"What's the scoop?" Lily asked.

"Scoop? Speaking of scooping, look over there," I said. But by the time I turned to where Alice had been scooping water, she was gone. "Never mind," I muttered. "Let's get away from these people."

"I want you to stay at Lily's house for the day," Mom said as Lily climbed into the Shannons' car. She was climbing into our beat-up Honda to drive to her shift at Wired. "I get off work at around three, and I'll come pick you up there."

"You don't have to do that," I said, feeling guilty

about making Mom go out of her way. "I can just take the number 66 back from Maple Leaf."

"But you'll have Mango with you," she pointed out.

"He can ride Metro. He just needs a ticket," I said. I guess Mom never realized that dogs could ride the bus. Working dogs—like guide dogs and service dogs — can ride for free, which makes total sense. Lapdogs can also ride for free. Big dogs, like Mango, pay full fare, which means he ends up paying more than I do for a "youth" ticket.

"That's good to know," Mom said. "But I'll still plan to come get you. Mango might not be as comfortable on public transportation as you are."

Dan drove the nearly four miles through city neighborhoods and the University of Washington area up to Maple Leaf, the neighborhood where Mom and I used to live before she was laid off from MegaComp. Those seemed like the good old days: We lived in a two-bedroom house with a nice yard and an alley that was perfect for skateboarding. Our house was just three blocks away from where Lily, my best friend since second grade at Olympic View Elementary, lives.

It's pretty fun to get to live in different parts of Seattle, especially when we get to live in rich people's neighborhoods, like a couple months ago when we lived downtown at the Belltown Towers. I doubted there were many soon-to-be-seventh graders in Seattle who lived on houseboats, too. Still, I'd give anything to be back in our old neighborhood with my friends nearby.

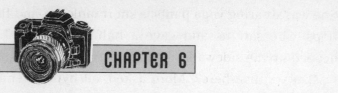

CHAPTER 6

THE WHITE CARGO VANS WERE PULLING OUT JUST AS WE RETURNED TO Portage Bay that afternoon. Mom pulled our Honda easily into a prime space close to the dock.

Mom, Mango, and I got out of our car and started walking slowly toward the dock.

A silver two-door hatchback with red tape over a taillight and music blaring out of the open windows came to a screeching halt on the street. The driver put the car into reverse and zipped into another prime parking space right in front of ours. The car's right rear wheel bumped up on the curb and onto the grass. The car pulled forward and thudded into the spot, then shuddered to a stop. It seemed so quiet as soon as the car stereo turned off.

I might be a few years away from my driver's license, but even I could tell that there was no reason to have to go over the curb.

The door creaked open and a woman with jet black hair in a high ponytail climbed out of the driver's seat. She was wearing yoga pants, a short tank top, and flip-flops. She saw us and gave a half smile, and then headed up the sidewalk to our dock.

"Do you live here?" Mom asked, all hyper-friendly, probably to make up for the judgmental thoughts she was trying to crowd out of her head. The ponytailed woman scowled at her.

"I don't mean to pry or anything," Mom said, talking superfast now. "It's just that we're house-sitting for one of the residents on this dock, and we haven't met the neighbors yet."

The woman kept walking toward the dock. "I'm just a house sitter, too," she said, not even looking at us.

I noticed the way she said "just" before "house sitter." Should I just resent her for making it sound as if Mom and I were low-lifes for living for free in someone else's home?

"Oh, what luck to catch you all at the same time!" Alice Campbell met us as we walked up the dock. "Maggie and Hannah, this is Estie Bartlett. She's taking care of Luci Mack's house and two cats for a couple of weeks."

Estie gave us another half smile. Wow. Add it to the

earlier one she gave us, and you'd have a whole smile. A forced smile, but a whole one.

"It's a rare occasion when we have two house sitters on our dock," Alice said. "That calls for a party. Or at least an informal gathering so you can meet all your neighbors."

"That sounds lovely," Mom said.

"I know you must be anxious to get back to your homes. I'm so sorry that the blasted film crew displaces us all during the day," Alice continued. She was a fast talker, but in a happy enthusiastic way.

"Didn't they allow anyone to stay at all?" I asked Alice. I tried to say it casually, but I wanted her to know I'd seen her on the film set.

"They insisted that everyone leave. That production assistant, Celeste, had me out of my own house first thing this morning. I spent most of the day at the downtown library. It was my day to volunteer as a tour guide. If you haven't toured the library, you simply must," Alice went on.

I noticed she hadn't directly answered my question. Yes, the crew of *Dockside Blues* had insisted that everyone leave. She also spent "most of the day" away. Was she just talking, or was she purposefully avoiding saying that she had been at the edge of the dock where the dead fish were?

"How did *Dockside Blues* end up on this particular dock?" Mom asked.

"Oh, the director has a connection. He grew up in Seattle, you know," Alice said. "Anyway, I hope you have some time to come over and join us on my deck this evening. The neighbors who are here are all anxious to meet you. Let's say six o'clock?"

"Great," Mom said. "What can we bring?"

"Oh, please. Just bring yourselves. We want to welcome you to the community," Alice said.

"I'll see if I'm feeling well enough to make it," the other house sitter said. She walked toward the first cottage on the left, unlocked the door, and quickly entered and closed the door behind her.

"I'll see you at six, then," Alice said. "Hannah, this could be a good opportunity for you to hand out your business cards to the other residents in the Floating Home Association. I'm sure some of your neighbors could use your help with errands or could recommend you as a dog walker for their friends. In any event, I'll see you in a few hours."

Mom and I continued on to our new home. Finally! Mango was practically jumping up and down, he was so excited to get back inside. Mom fumbled with the keys until she unlocked the shiny purple door. She held the door open for me. Mango took off, immediately going inside to reclaim his territory and chase his cat. I was still hyperaware of the motion of being on the water. It felt weird—being in the safety of a house while it moves. Still, I was pretty sure I could get used to this walking-on-water business.

CHAPTER 7

"HANNAH? HANNAH? WAKE UP, DEAR," A VOICE FROM FAR, FAR AWAY seemed to be calling to me.

I tried to push it out of my dreams, but it came back. "Hannah?"

I woke up with a start. Not only was I in a strange bed sleeping with a huge beast, but a total stranger was nudging me awake.

"I'm awake!" I said as convincingly as I could.

I pushed myself up on one elbow and looked around to get my bearings. Okay. I was in the bedroom/office in Jake Heard's houseboat. The beast next to me was a drooling labradoodle named Mango. I glanced at my disco clock radio that I'd set next to the bed and saw that it was 6:30 at night. And Alice Campbell was waking me from a pretty darn good dream that I'm pretty sure included tin roof sundaes on a gently rocking boat.

"I didn't mean to startle you, but I wanted to make sure you and Mango make it to the dockside party," she said.

"Right," I said slowly.

"I've been meaning to tell you something," Alice said. That got my attention. I sat up immediately. Mango got up, too, and went into that downward dog yoga pose that is possibly one of the most aptly named maneuvers in the world.

"I wanted to tell you my whole name," Alice continued. "It's Alice Kawamoto Campbell."

She must have seen the "ah-ha" moment in my eyes.

"You were wondering, weren't you?" she asked.

I nodded. "I thought maybe you were Japanese, but I wasn't sure, and then I was kind of embarrassed that I even wondered."

"You should never be embarrassed to ask what you want to know. I would have understood if you'd asked me if I were Japanese. Or whatever. Just like I'd like to ask you if you're Chinese."

"Yep. Born in China. Adopted by Maggie and moved to Seattle. Was Kawamoto your maiden name?" I asked.

"It was, and it is. It is still my family name. Now I use it as my middle name. I keep it safe between my first and last names."

I liked that. I was liking Alice Kawamoto Campbell.

Then I remembered that she was sneaking around the set of *Dockside Blues* and at the island nation of Tui Tui. She was up to something, and I wanted to know what. Would it be rude to ask? Or worse, would I be asking something I really didn't want to know the answer to? I wasn't so sure I wanted to know if this nice woman was involved in something shady.

"Hannah, please remember that if you want to know something, you need only to ask. I'll tell you what I can," she said.

Did she really mean it? I wasn't so sure. "Did you say party?" I asked, standing.

Alice smiled at me. "We're just firing up the barbecue. Follow me."

The Portage Bay dock party would have been a total bore if it wasn't on the water. Maybe rich people in general are total bores, but we don't always notice right away because the packaging and surroundings are interesting. Nah. I had to swallow that ugly, jealous thought. I have a tendency to resent people with money for the simple fact that they have money. And we don't.

There might even be interesting people right there, but all the adults were talking about the Floating Home

Association and committees and something-or-other about action with so-and-so on the city council. I tuned it all out and sat in a comfy high-back wood deck chair with a lemonade slushy and my camera. I had a fresh roll of 36-exposure black-and-white film, and I'd promised Lily I'd get photos of any celebrities who might stop by. Just in case.

"Estie! I'm delighted you could join us!" Alice said. She handed a glass of iced tea to the other house sitter. With my well-developed and always subtle eavesdropping skills, I learned that Estie had been living there for about a week. She was taking care of two cats and she was a yoga teacher at one of those sweaty yoga places, where they keep the room superwarm.

"Who invited him?" Frank, the owner of the red cottage, asked, scowling at the sunglasses-clad man striding toward the dock.

"Oh, I did, Frank! We need more excitement around here," said Louisa, the woman from the blue cottage.

"Of course we do," Alice murmured.

Estie smoothed her tight pink T-shirt and tucked it in. She used her free hand to fluff her hair.

"Welcome, Marcus!" Louisa did that Hollywood kiss-kiss thing with Marcus Dartmouth, director, *Dockside Blues*.

"Aunt Alice! Always a pleasure to see you," Marcus said, giving Alice a stiff hug and pat on the back.

Did he say *aunt*? I stared at Alice.

"Marcus, I think you know most of my neighbors here," Alice said, "But let me introduce you to Estie Bartlett. She's house-sitting for Luci Mack."

"Yes, we met earlier today," Marcus said, extending his hand toward Mom. Estie looked crestfallen.

"I'm actually Maggie West. My daughter and I are house-sitting for Jake Heard at the end of the dock," Mom said. I could tell she was amused.

"Maggie, this is my nephew, Marc. Excuse me, *Marcus*. And Marcus, this is Maggie, and *this* is Estie," Alice said.

Marcus recovered his goof quickly, but he looked rather confused. Estie was practically glowing as she enthusiastically pumped Marcus's hand.

"I'm such a fan of your work, Mr. Dartmouth," she said. She said it like *Dart-mouth*, not *Dart-muth*, which is the way Marcus Dartmouth, director, *Dockside Blues*, says it.

"Please, call me" —I waited for him to say something like "Call me Marcus," but instead he finished— "*Mr. Dart-muth*." He pronounced it for her. He handed her his card and—I swear I saw this—winked at her. Estie, who was already showing a deep blush of embarrassment under her golden tan, turned even redder.

"Aunt Alice, have you seen Mum and Timothy lately?" Marcus asked. I swear I heard it just like that—he actually said "mum."

"No, dear, but I imagine you could probably catch them at the Emerald City Yacht Club on an evening like this," she said. "If they're not on the water, they're probably working on the *Clean Sweep*."

"Yes, I suppose I could drive down there and see," he said. "Although they might put me to work cleaning the bottom of that boat."

"Drive? It's just four blocks away! You've spent too much time in L.A. if you think you can't walk down the street," Frank's voice boomed. "Heck, you could jump in right here and swim down there. Might do you some good. Help you cool off and all that."

"I don't think I'd want to swim in that water right now," Louisa said.

"Frank! Please don't encourage anyone to go swimming in this water!" Alice said sternly.

"Were there really dead fish in the water today?" I asked.

Marcus took off his sunglasses and looked at me. His expression seemed to say, Who are you and why are you talking to me?

"I heard that actress, Monica, say she touched dead fish," I added.

"Monica has a tendency to overact sometimes. She is, after all, an actress," Marcus said.

"Yes, she is quite the actress," Estie said. "Always has been."

"There's nothing wrong with the water. The water is perfectly safe." Marcus stated it as if he was at a press conference on the TV news.

"She sounded pretty convincing," I said. "I mean, she really screams well."

Marcus tried to laugh. Only thing was, I wasn't trying to be funny.

CHAPTER 8

"LILY! ANSWER IF YOU'RE THERE." I WAITED FOR A FEW SECONDS. "Okay. Listen. The TV crew is going to be here again tomorrow at nine. See if you can get a ride down here before they start setting up. I have a plan."

I closed my cell phone and plugged it into the charger. Mom was on the deck, reading and watching the boats go by. I picked up my camera and headed out to join her. I had taken only a couple of photos at the dockside barbecue, and they were pretty uninspired. I was itching to experiment with the fading evening light and the long shadows that reached out into the lake water.

"Isn't this incredible?" Mom asked, putting her book down on the table. "If I block out the traffic noise from the bridge, I feel as if we're on a raft in the middle of the water. And all the boaters are so friendly." Mom waved to a motorboat and five shirtless teenage boys waved back.

"Did you have to wave to them?" I asked, mortified.

"I believe the friendly wave is part of the boating culture," she said. "I think they wave so they have an excuse for staring at the people on their decks and houseboats."

I fiddled with the camera's telephoto lens and looked through the viewfinder. I took a quick glance at the boys in the boat, but then kept the lens moving so Mom wouldn't think I was checking out boys.

"I wonder why so many boats are coming by right now," I said.

"We're close to the Emerald City Yacht Club, just a few blocks away. My guess is that people spent the day out in Lake Union or in the Puget Sound and they're heading back now that the sun is setting," Mom said.

"Is that the same yacht club that Marcus Dartmouth, director, mentioned?"

Mom granted me a laugh for the way I tried to say "Marcus Dartmouth, director" like I was a Hollywood hotshot. "Yes, it is. Alice told me that Marcus grew up on the other side of the arboretum, in a gated neighborhood called Broadmoor. Apparently his mother and stepfather have been big boaters since he was a young boy. Perhaps I should say they're 'yachters.'"

"What makes a boat a yacht?" I asked. "'Yacht' sounds so uppity."

"Attitude," Mom said.

"Huh?"

"Attitude is what makes a boat a yacht, although yacht owners might say that a boat has to be a certain length to be deemed a true yacht." Mom reached for her laptop, and I picked up my camera and focused on a sailboat coming past us. I might be an obsessive artist, but my mom is beyond obsessive when it comes to checking things online. I knew I was about to be in for a definition of "yacht."

"Interesting," she said. "There doesn't seem to be one singular definition for 'yacht.' One dictionary says a yacht is a 'large usually motor-driven craft used for pleasure cruising.' It doesn't give a specific size. But some people claim that a vessel must be longer than thirty feet to be a yacht. Still others insist that it must be longer than sixty-five feet, or somewhere between sixty-five and one hundred fifty feet."

"Yowza. Those are some big boats they're talking about," I said.

"You mean *yachts*. It goes back to my original observation: It's all about attitude."

Now I had a front-row seat to watch this boating, sailing, and yachting crowd. I picked up the camera again, moving the lens from boat to boat. There wasn't any wind, so even the sailboats had to use motors to putter through the bay. I clicked a photo of a large motorboat—probably long enough to qualify as a yacht—with wood trim. The name *Clean Sweep* was painted in an ornate style on the side. A man in a captain's hat sat in the driver's seat, puttering along. He killed the engine and let the boat rock gently in the wake of the other boats. An older woman with bright blond hair peered at the exterior side of the boat. I took another picture just as she grimaced. The man shook his head and lifted a large plastic bucket and sat it on the bench seat in the back. The woman used a smaller plastic bucket to scoop something out. She leaned far over the side of the boat and dropped something in the water. The man nudged her and pointed over to us. I quickly lowered the camera and gave a big, friendly boating wave.

They didn't wave back.

CHAPTER 9

THE NEXT MORNING I AWOKE TO A WET NOSE AND THE SOUND OF TAP-
dancing toenails. Mango needed to go to the bathroom.

"You're such a polite dog," I told him as I hooked his
retractable leash to his collar. Instead of barking for
attention, Mango seemed to like to do a little potty
dance on the wood floor of the houseboat. It must be
the Standard poodle in him.

Mom had already left to work the breakfast shift
at Wired Café downtown. As I walked out of our
houseboat, two newspapers, the *New York Times* and
the *Seattle Times*, were waiting on our welcome mat.
Pretty spiffy aim if the paper carrier could land the
newspapers right on our doorstep without veering off
into the water. I took the blue plastic wrapper from the
New York Times just in case I needed a poop bag.
Mango was high-stepping down the wood dock, obviously anxious to get to the small grassy patch by the

mailboxes. "We're almost there, fella," I said to the dog.

"Good morning!" the neighbor who I think was named Frank called out to us. "Mango taking you out to stretch your legs?" He was watering the flowers in the dozen or more planters arranged on his deck.

I nodded and held up the blue plastic bag from the newspaper.

Frank laughed. "Glad to see you got your paper and that you have multiple uses for it. The papers come to the mailboxes around five in the morning. I bring them all up after my six o'clock run."

"Wow. That's nice. Thanks."

"No problem."

Mango and I walked along Boyer Avenue. We stopped at the Canal Market because one of us was enticed by a pink-frosted doughnut from the extra-yummy Top Pot bakery. The other one of us waited outside patiently for a doggie treat. We turned around and passed our dock, continuing down several blocks until I came to the forbidding entrance to the Emerald City Yacht Club.

"Oh, excuse me!" I said, jumping back as the locked gate swung open and almost slammed into my face.

"Yes," said the woman who came out from the private yacht club. Was she saying, "Yes, excuse you"?

That wasn't very polite. I'd try to make up for her lack of small-talk skills with some extra polite talk of my own.

"Gorgeous morning for boating. Are you just going out?"

"No," she said. She was holding the gate open and glancing behind her.

"Come on, Timothy," she said.

"Coming, Stella," came a voice, along with a man in a captain's hat whom I recognized from last night.

"I believe I saw you in your boat last night," I said.

"It's a yacht," the woman said.

"Right. I think I saw you in your yacht right before sunset. It's gorgeous."

"If you think these compliments will get you a ride on the *Clean Sweep*, you'll have to come back another day." The man smiled affably at me. "I just docked her after our morning, er, our morning . . . "

Now he seemed to be stumbling for words.

"Our morning errand," the woman finished for him. "Give me the bag." He handed her an open-top canvas tote bag. As she quickly rummaged through it, I saw a glimpse of what looked like a black Gore-tex rain jacket and rain pants. I tried to picture her wearing them.

"Took a while to get her cleaned up," Timothy was saying. "The plants are pretty thick in the lake right now. They wreak havoc on the hull. But we got her all tidy, and she's as gorgeous as ever now," the man said. I assumed he was still talking about his boat. Or yacht. Whatever. He was pretty nice, but my attention was focused on her. This was the third time I'd seen this same woman. I was sure she'd been on our dock when we first moved in and yesterday morning when the TV crew was setting up.

"Well, good-bye then," I said, attempting another friendly boating wave as they walked off.

Once again, I didn't get a wave back. So much for the friendly, waving boating crowd. Make that *yachting* crowd.

As Mango and I were returning from our walk, I spotted Lily and her dad.

"Hannah!" Lily hopped off the hood of her dad's car and came rushing over to us. "My parents said I can stay here with you all day."

"Lily, call us before dinner," her dad called. "Stay dry, girls."

"I thought your dad would want to see our house-boat," I said as Dan Shannon drove off.

"He's dying to see it. But he's on his way to meet a bunch of people for some big bike ride for the Cascade

Bicycle Club," she said. "So what's the plan? I hope it's about how to get onto *Dockside Blues*. You have to tell me everything Marcus Dartmouth said last night. Whoa! Who's that doing those power yoga moves?"

"Doing what?" I followed Lily's finger, which was pointing to the first cottage on the left. Inside, Estie was doing some kind of handstand maneuver. Her body was in an upside-down crouching position with all her weight balanced on her hands. She stayed motionless.

"That's the heron position. Or crane. Or some kind of bird," Lily whispered. "I saw it in a yoga book. Who's the yogini?"

"She's another house sitter," I said. As I said it, the word "sister" almost came spilling out. House sitter. Sister. "Maybe she's the sister house sitter that director dude was talking about," I said.

"Which would make her Monica Heathcliff's sister! Which would make her a good person for us to get to know if we want to get a role on *Dockside Blues*."

"I dunno. Her name is Estie Bartlett, not Estie Heathcliff," I said.

"Oh, come on! Heathcliff is so obviously a made-up name. It's so obvious it's almost embarrassing for the person who thought it up," Lily said, smiling.

"And Estie's hair is black, but Monica's is blond."

"And I'd bet that neither color is natural," Lily said.

"Good morning!" Alice Campbell was just getting out of her bright red kayak. She pulled a black soft-side cooler out from the cargo area. I stooped down to help her lift the kayak out of the water.

"Thank you! It's so much easier with two people." She dried her hands on her pants and held one out to Lily. "Nice to see you again, Lily."

"It's tough, but as Hannah's best friend, I'm obligated to stand by her during this incredibly difficult time while she's living on a houseboat," Lily said.

Alice laughed. "I'm afraid we'll have another day of film crew disruptions in our midst today. Marcus assures me there will be only a few days on location here. They'll do the rest back at the studio in Los Angeles."

I saw Lily's eyebrows go up with interest as Alice referred to the director, Marcus, so casually.

"Is Marcus really your nephew?" I blurted out.

"He is, indeed. You seem surprised."

"He just doesn't seem like he'd be related to you. He's not as nice. No offense to your nephew or anything," I added hurriedly.

Luckily, Alice laughed. "I thought you were going to say we don't look alike," she said. "Marcus is good underneath that Hollywood act of his. He's always been special to me. His father was my husband's brother. Unfortunately, both of the Campbell brothers died in a car accident many years ago. Marcus's mother, Stella, immediately remarried. Marcus was adopted by his stepfather, Timothy Dartmouth."

Okay. I'm not dense. I'd already figured that the man and woman I'd seen seen at the yacht club were Marcus's parents. Or at least I assumed they were. How many couples named Stella and Timothy could there be who have a boat—er, excuse me, a *yacht*—called the *Clean Sweep*?

"His parents really like to keep their boat ship-shape, don't they? They were already cleaning it this morning," I said.

Alice gave me a sharp glance. Her tone of voice was markedly different as she said, "You saw the *Clean Sweep*? When? Where was it? Do you remember what time?"

Whoa on the barrage of questions. "Um, I saw it last night when it was getting dark. It was out there," I pointed. "I think they were out this morning, too. Mango and I just ran into them when they were leaving Emerald City Yacht Club."

"So they were already out this morning, were they? I was out on the water by seven, but I didn't see them. I'll have to get up earlier next time. What time do you think it was when they returned?"

I told her I'd seen them on the land, so I didn't really know. I wasn't at all sure why it was important. "Good, good. This is all good information, Hannah," Alice said distractedly. "Quite useful information." She grabbed the soft-side cooler and I heard glass jars clanking against one another inside. She was mumbling to herself, something about levels and minutes and evaporation. Alice looked me in the eyes. "Hannah, please tell me if you see the *Clean Sweep* again."

And with that, she quickly went into her houseboat and shut the door, leaving me with all sorts of questions spinning through my head. Why would Alice want to know if I saw Marcus Dartmouth's parents? Was she trying to hide something from them? Or were they hiding something from her? I suspected that Stella and Timothy were dumping something in the water. I've heard about lakes and ponds that are "stocked" with fish. People actually put fish into the water so that fishermen have better chances of catching something. Was it possible that Marcus's parents were trying to stock this part of the lake? Maybe they'd chosen the wrong kind of fish or something.

Oh, ick. Maybe they were dumping dead fish in the lake.

Nah, that's crazy.

CHAPTER 10

"I'M NOT QUITE FOLLOWING ALL THIS," LILY SAID, AS MANGO LED US down the L-shaped dock to our cottage. I filled her in as best I could.

"If these people have a yacht four blocks away and she wants to see them, why doesn't she just go down there? Why does she have you on the lookout for this boat?" Lily asked.

"Plus, they're related. That makes it even weirder," I added.

Lily had me fill her in on every single word Marcus Dartmouth, director, had said the night before. None of it was terribly interesting, yet she hung onto every word.

"Did anyone last night say anything about needing extras? Because, you know, I'm here and ready to work," Lily said.

"I don't know. I had a feeling that the other house

sitter is hoping for a role, too. I'm thinking that if they want this show to be a success, they'd cast Mango," I said, rewarding the dog with a belly rub since he was looking especially cute. "Maybe there's a part for him."

Do you think that other house sitter has a chance at a role?" she asked.

"I have no idea."

"I wonder if they'd put Mango's name in the credits," Lily mused. "Maybe I should change my name. You know, have a better stage name. Lily Newman. Lily Pacino. Lily Lang, Lily . . . "

A rap on the wood frame of the cottage door interrupted Lily and sent Mango into a series of barks.

"Hello? I need to ask for your cooperation this morning," a high-pitched voice called from the doorway. I hadn't even said "come in" or anything when Celeste, the production assistant, walked inside. "Yes, yes, Joshua. I have it all under control. I'll use the Polaroids." I looked behind her to see where Joshua was, and then I realized she was having two conversations at once: one with us and the other on the headset of her cell phone.

"Now, girls, here are the Polaroids of the set from yesterday. I need to close the blinds to the exact same degree as in this shot." She handed a photograph to me.

"See what you can do to match this photo. Then you're free to leave."

Lily and I stared at her. She sighed. "Please. *Please* see if you can match this photo," she said. "I'm sorry if I sound snappish, but Joshua is such a demanding continuity guy. We have to finish the shots we didn't get yesterday because, because . . . because Miss Heathcliff needed to leave early."

"Yeah, I heard she had a spa emergency. Ow!" Lily kicked me along the side of my leg, nailing my anklebone. "Watch it," I muttered to her.

"You watch it," she whispered.

Celeste was fighting back a smile. She regained her stony-faced production assistant look and got all businesslike again. "Monica was a little concerned because she thought she touched something dead in the water," Celeste said. "You know how sometimes seaweed or leaves touch your toes in the water and it spooks you. That's all it was. Anyway, girls, if you could help me out, it would be great. Oh, and don't forget that you need to be out of here before we start filming."

She pivoted around on spikey heeled flip-flops. Two steps down the dock and one of the heels went down between two wood planks, sending her sprawling. Like we didn't see that one coming.

I rushed over to her and helped her up. "Are you okay?"

"I'm okay. Embarrassed, but okay." She took off her flip-flops and hurled them into the water, immediately bursting into a fit of giggles. Lily and I exchanged looks. I'm pretty independent, but I am in no position to deal with some random adult's mental illness or emotional breakdown.

"Um, do you want us to try to get your shoes out of the water?" I asked. Mango crouched in his classic downward dog yoga pose at the edge of the dock, wagging his tail and eyeing one of Celeste's sandals as if it were a tennis ball waiting for retrieval.

"No, thanks. They were stupid shoes anyway. I bought them last night just to try to look more, more . . . I don't know what more I was looking for actually," she said, getting up to her feet and dusting off her white pants. "Maybe I was hoping uncomfortable shoes would make me act tougher or something."

"Uncomfortable shoes just make me whine," I said. Lily had grabbed a kayak paddle and was trying to move the shoes closer to her.

"You can have them if you get them," Celeste told her. "I've got some sneakers in my car. I'll be more human in my own shoes."

Celeste's bare feet padded gingerly along the wood dock back to the street.

"Fetch, Mango!" Lily instructed the Labrador retriever and poodle mix. Instantly the dog made a splash into the water and headed for one of the sandals.

"Lily! Why did you do that? Now Celeste will get in trouble because the dock is wet and that Joshua guy will yell at her and maybe even fire her," I said.

"It's a dock! Docks get wet." She accepted one of the sandals from Mango's mouth and told him to fetch the other one. He happily turned around and continued his mission.

"We're going to have to wash the dog again," I whined.

"Oops, hadn't thought of that," Lily admitted. "But didn't Celeste just say that there was nothing to worry about?" She leaned over the edge of the dock again.

"Well, unlike you, I don't want to take any chances," I told her.

"Eureka!" Lily cried triumphantly, holding up both sandals. "Oh, and look! They fit!"

"Oh, and look . . . they look ridiculous," I added.

Mango made a move like he was about to shake, and I immediately backed up. No offense to the dog, but I didn't want any suspicious water drops on me, either. Alice had been so adamant about washing lake water off of him. If it was bad for the pooch, I bet it was bad for humans, too. "We need to get this dog washed," I said to Lily. She was still eyeing her feet and the sandals admiringly.

"The problem is, you have no eye for fashion," Lily said.

"I think we have a bigger problem right now," I said.

"Celeste was so nice to give these to me," Lily said.

"She is actually pretty nice," I said. "That's why I feel bad for what we're about to do."

CHAPTER 11

"WHAT? WE'RE GOING TO DO NOTHING? THAT SEEMS SO BORING. Especially coming from you," Lily said. I'd filled her in on my plan while we washed Mango off in the shower. Now Lily was pivoting in half circles, admiring her new high-heeled sandals in front of the closet mirror upstairs in Jake's bedroom loft.

"Nothing. Absolutely nothing. You see, if we stay inside here, we can watch all the action firsthand. I thought you'd like that."

"I don't want to *watch* the action. I want to be on TV," Lily said.

"Really?" I used my best fake-astonishment voice. "Actually, Lily, nothing is brilliant." I had to pause and think through what I'd said. I'm not often making philosophical proclamations like that. "What I mean is, doing nothing is brilliant. The more we know about the script, the characters, and how things work, the easier it will be for us to get Marcus Dartmouth, director, to put us on the show."

"Us? You want to be on *Dockside Blues*, too?"

"You bet. I think they need some diversity on that show, based on all the white people we saw on the dock yesterday. Shhh! Someone's coming. Darn. I guess we're stuck here now."

"Darn," Lily said, smiling.

We crawled silently to the window, peering between two slats in the white blinds on the loft window. Two black-hooded shapes moved quickly along the dock, glancing behind them several times.

"Hold on," I whispered to Lily. I tiptoed down to my bedroom and grabbed my camera and an extra lens. Back upstairs, I put on the telephoto lens and wedged the long lens through the slats of the blinds and adjusted the focus until I could see the two faces crystal clear. Despite their melodramatic entrance and head movements, I knew they couldn't be part of the TV show. Unless Marcus Dartmouth had decided to give his mother and stepfather a couple of stealthy roles and they were rehearsing before the film crew arrived.

"What are they pouring out?" Lily whispered.

I took a couple of photographs. "It's not dead fish.

Not even nondead fish," I said, backing away from the window, suddenly feeling overwhelmingly sad. "I'm afraid it might be something to kill fish, though. Something toxic."

We had just witnessed Timothy and Stella Dartmouth walking along the outer edge of the dock, each shaking a plastic bucket so that a white powder spewed into the water. It looked like laundry detergent, but I had a feeling it wasn't quite that simple. I hadn't seen what they'd emptied into the lake from their boat the other night, but I bet it was the same substance. I couldn't imagine what it was, but if we could figure that out, maybe we could figure out why the Dartmouths were pouring it into Lake Washington.

"We need to get a sample of the water as soon as possible," I said.

"And then what, Captain Science? Do we run some of our genius scientific experiments in our basement laboratory? Oops. We forgot to make a secret laboratory in the basement. Double oops! The basement of this houseboat would be underwater and kind of wet."

"Shhh!" I said as I watched Stella and Timothy skulk away in their matching black, hooded rain gear. Someone should tell them that villains use black *at night* because it helps them blend in. Head-to-toe black clothing on a sunny Seattle day was hardly going with the flow in terms of wardrobe choice.

Before I could even leave the loft window perch, another person came on the dock. Still not someone from *Dockside Blues*.

"What's she doing out here?" Lily whispered.

Estie, the other houseboat house sitter, peered around the corner of the Morrisons' cottage and then stepped out to the far side of the dock. She set down a fishing tackle box and swiftly plopped herself into a cross-legged sitting position. Then, just as quickly, she unfurled her legs, snapped the tackle box closed, and took refuge behind the gate at the Morrisons' cottage.

Alice Campbell came out on the dock, doing the same quiet walk and furtive glancing over her shoulder as the previous dockside visitors. She opened a thermal cooler bag and took out two jars. She took another look behind her and then began pouring something from one jar to the other. Then she dumped the mixture into the lake water. She took another jar out of the cooler and used it to scoop up some water. Then she took a fourth jar out of the cooler, unscrewed the top, and poured from this jar into the third jar. Alice closed all the jars, placed them carefully back in the black bag, and zipped the cooler shut.

As soon as Alice left, Estie was back on the dock with her tackle box. Why in the world were all these people so interested in the water here? Were they messing it up or cleaning it up? And why all the scurrying?

At that point, the setup crew arrived, and I suddenly understood why everyone was rushing around.

"We shouldn't have gone through the drive-thru at Starbucks," a man said as he and another man rolled a cart of equipment onto the dock. "It always takes longer to go through the drive-thru than to go inside and wait in the line. It's also a waste of gas."

As they approached, Estie hurriedly put her jars and bottles back in the tackle box.

"No, no," the second man said. "It wastes more gas to turn off the engine and restart it."

"That's ridiculous. There's no way it could use more gas to go inside—"

A clatter of glass interrupted their debate when they came upon Estie, who was holding the open tackle box by the handle, while the contents rolled along the dock.

"Good thing nothing broke," one of the men said. "Joshua and Marcus wouldn't take too kindly to the dock being wet where it wasn't wet yesterday."

I grimaced, noticing that Mango's wet splashes were still visible on the dock.

"Sorry!" Estie said, grabbing bottles and scooping them back in her box.

"No harm done," the taller guy said. "But everyone should be off the dock before Marcus gets here."

Estie smoothed down her hair with her right hand. "Are you expecting Marcus soon?"

"Any minute. For some reason he wants to be here during setup today."

"I'll get out of your way then," Estie said.

"You look familiar," the other guy said. "Were you ever on *Love Today*? Not that I ever watched the daytime dramas."

"Ha! Anyone who says 'daytime drama' instead of 'soap opera' is definitely someone who watches them," the first man said.

The second guy shoved him a bit. "Nah. I didn't watch them. I could have worked on them though, you know. Been on the crew or something." They kept bickering as they started opening crates and unzipping black bags that protected equipment. Estie smiled and tossed her long dark hair over her right shoulder and walked back to her cottage, swishing her hips and holding the tackle box like it was a patent leather handbag.

"Exit stage left," Lily said as we watched Estie

almost prance down the dock as if she were a model on a runway.

Watching a crew set up for a television show is possibly the dullest thing imaginable. In fact, I don't think it's even imaginable. I have a pretty darn good imagination, and I am confident I can't imagine something that dull. After ten minutes of absolute nothingness—just a lot of unloading of equipment and screwing poles together—we decided to take a silent-TV break. We watched an episode of *Full House* with the closed-captioning on. Twenty-eight minutes later—and the crew still wasn't completely set up.

"TV is boring," I said.

"Hey! Don't make fun of Michelle and D.J. and Joey, and I won't make fun of your Crime Channel addiction," Lily said. Lily proudly claims to have watched *Full House* reruns every week since she was four years old and often talks about the Danny Tanner family as if they were her next-door neighbors.

"I meant that making a TV show is boring," I explained. "The only thing possibly more boring is watching people make a TV show."

"Let me know when the good stuff starts," Lily said, not taking her eyes off the TV screen as another episode of *Full House* started. I sighed and went back to scoping things out through my camera lens. I moved the lens down the dock until I settled on the golden, shiny head of Monica Heathcliff, the star of *Dockside Blues*, who was in a heated argument with another woman. Both women stood with their hands on their hips, occasionally pointing a hand at the other woman.

I gently eased the window open a crack in the hope of hearing what they were talking about.

"You need to keep your hands out of my business," Monica said.

"It's all over now. They're dead," the other woman said, her voice loud and shrill.

"They're all dead, and there's nothing you can do to bring them back, Celeste."

CHAPTER 12

"CELESTE?" LILY ROLLED OFF THE BED WITH A THUD AND CRAWLED TO our lookout spot.

Unfortunately, her thudding upstairs disturbed Mango from his peaceful slumber downstairs.

Mango's barking was interrupted by Marcus Dartmouth shouting, "Cut! Cut! Who let a dog stay here during filming? Joshua? Where's Celeste? Wasn't she responsible for clearing everyone out?"

"Oops," Lily said. "I didn't know they were filming yet. Wasn't Monica just yelling at Celeste?"

I sighed. A big, heavy sigh, as if to say, You have so much to learn. Then I said, "It appears that 'Celeste' is also the name of a character who was just doing a scene with Monica Heathcliff. A scene that you interrupted."

"Double oops. I thought there was something dead in the water again," Lily replied, and I sighed again dramatically. Clearly Lily needed to watch different television shows to keep up with the real-life show going on below.

"Okay, boy, let's go face the music," I said to Mango. He wagged his tail, excited to go outside.

"I'm sorry, Mr. Dartmouth, sir," I said as I opened the front door to our cottage. Eight adults were looking directly at me, and not one of them looked happy.

"Marcus! I am exhausted, and I have no patience for continually having to redo scenes out here." Monica Heathcliff looked positively furious. "We need to wrap this up and get out of this waterlogged world and get back to L.A. I insist that you take care of things."

Marcus rolled his eyes and started barking orders for the crew as he walked away.

"Don't you walk away from me," Monica shouted at him. "Come here! Now!"

Hearing those three words, Mango's ears perked up, and he lunged toward Monica.

"Mango! No!" I cried. But it was too late. The dog bounded toward Monica. He's sweet and smart, but he must have honed in on her last few words, thinking she was urgently commanding him to "come here, now."

I charged after him, and Monica threw her hands in

the air and started to back away as Mango neared, then jumped up on her.

"Mango! Down! Off! Off!" I couldn't remember if I was supposed to say "down" to get off or "off" to get off. I grabbed him by his collar, but he got up on his hind legs again as if he were dancing with the actress. I had never seen Mango jump up on anyone like that—her hand movements must have been giving him some sort of "up" signal.

Monica continued to stagger backward away from him, and I grabbed for his collar again, shouting, "Down, Mango, down!"

And down he went—pushing the actress who, according to Lily, *People* magazine had recently named one of the Ten Hot New Stars to Watch, with him—and into the water. Unfortunately, my fingers had finally managed to hook his collar, so I went in, too.

"Aaaaarrrgh! Help! Get me out of here! There were dead things in here yesterday!" Monica flailed her arms around, splashing water frantically.

"Here, Miss Heathcliff," I said, treading water. "Take my arm." I bent my arm and held it out so she could steady herself. "Just take a couple strokes down here. There's a ladder." She came along with me, sputtering and spitting and crying all at the same time. Black globs of mascara ran down her cheeks. I guided her to the ladder and then backed up so she could get out first. She was practically hyperventilating she was crying so hard now. "Don't look at me! Don't anyone look at me! That awful dog! He attacked me for no reason!"

"Sorry," I squeaked. "I think he thought you were calling him."

As she climbed up the ladder, Monica bent her arm so that her elbow and forearm covered the top of her face. The TV people stood around gawking at her. Only Lily ventured forward, helping her up the ladder. Once Monica was all the way up on the dock, she took her arms and covered her chest. Celeste—the real Celeste—draped a huge blanket over Monica Heathcliff's shoulders. Two other women guided her off the dock and to one of the trailers out on the street.

Everything was eerily silent. I sensed that the entire cast and crew of *Dockside Blues* were holding their breath.

Marcus Dartmouth's laughter cut through the air like a gas-powered leaf blower roaring into action. "That was priceless! Did you get all of that, Roxy?"

A woman peeked out from behind the camera. "Oh yeah. I got it, all right."

"I couldn't have scripted this better myself. Celeste! I mean the *real* Celeste, the P.A. Celeste! Where are you?" Marcus demanded.

Celeste stepped forward, looking as if she was going to barf.

"Celeste, I want you to find out who owns this dog and get permission for him to join the cast of *Dockside Blues*. You! Up on the dock!" he said, motioning toward me.

Being up on the dock getting chewed out by a TV director was the absolute last place I wanted to be.

Until I turned around and saw the fish. The dead fish.

And then the water was the absolute last place I wanted to be.

"Mango! Let's go, boy!" I said.

CHAPTER 13

"ICK! ICK, ICK, ICK!" I TOOK SIX FREESTYLE STROKES TO THE LADDER, keeping my head above water. I pulled myself up a couple of rungs, panting heavily. "Come on, Mango! Lily, help me get Mango out of the water! We need to get him out of the water!" I was panicking. If something killed fish, who knows what it could do to Mango. Or to me. Alice had been so adamant that we wash the dog if he got lake water on him. Why hadn't she just told me what was wrong with the water?

My heart seemed to lurch at the same time my brain was whizzing at full speed. Maybe Alice hadn't told us anything specific because she was the one who was doing something weird to the water. No time to think about that. Mango and I had to get clean.

One of the guys who'd unloaded the equipment earlier bent over and effortlessly hauled Mango up on the dock. "Back away!" I commanded. "He's about to shake." Amazingly, people did what I said. Everyone took a couple steps back, as if Mango was some kind of weapon that was going to explode. Mango started to do his predictable wet-dog shake to start getting the water off him.

"There's something wrong with the water here. I just saw dead fish. And Monica saw dead fish yesterday," I explained. Mango sat down and looked at me with his head cocked. "It's okay, boy. We'll get you a bath." I don't know if it was my imagination, but he didn't look too excited about the bath idea.

"Well, I don't see any dead fish," Marcus proclaimed, having glanced over the side of the dock into the water.

"Well, I did!" I said, trying to imitate his tone, with the emphasis on "I," because *I* am just as important as he is.

"You might think you saw dead fish, but it was probably just some plant floating by," Marcus said.

"Monica saw dead fish, too," Lily said, handing a beach towel to me and wrapping a second towel around Mango.

"Monica Heathcliff is an actress. An actress must act. That's what she was doing yesterday—acting," he said.

No one seemed to challenge him on that one. No one was agreeing either.

"I know what I saw," I said, looking directly at Marcus. "There were dead fish in the water, and earlier I saw your parents—"

"Aunt Alice," Marcus said as he quickly turned away from me. "How delightful of you to stop by." He said "aunt" like "aaaaahnt," instead of like "ant." It sounded phony. Then again, this is a guy who calls his mom "mum."

"I live here, Marcus. Or did you forget? I seem to be kicked out of my home while you work on this project of yours." Alice Campbell turned from Marcus and looked directly at me. "Hannah, you need to get into a shower right away. Wash yourself first, and then you girls need to get Mango in the bathtub and give him a thorough shower, too. Here, I brought some special soap for you to use on him."

"Aunt Alice, we're in the middle of something here. I'm sure the girl's and the dog's baths can wait," Marcus said.

"And *I'm* sure they can't wait," Alice said. "You should know that as well as I do." They stared at each other.

I looked from Marcus to Alice. Neither one said

anything. Neither one flinched. I was certain that Alice believed something was in the water that wasn't supposed to be there. Something that could kill fish.

And now I had a feeling that Marcus knew, too. I had a feeling Marcus knew exactly what was going on.

"Hannah, I encourage you to get cleaned up," Alice urged me. "I can help you, if you'd like."

"No!" The thought of someone helping me get clean caused instant and thorough mortification. "I mean, no, thank you."

She smiled kindly. "I meant I could help you with Mango. But I know you're an experienced dog washer. Just make sure you rinse him thoroughly. Try to rinse him twice as long as you think is necessary. And be sure to get his belly, his face, and his ears. Inside his ears as well."

Thirty minutes later and Lily was as wet as I was. Washing a dog Mango's size is no easy matter, especially when the usually obedient dog was getting a little testy, seeing as how we were washing him even more thoroughly this time. Alice had me a little alarmed about what chemicals might be in the water at Portage Bay. And let's not forget that I'd actually seen dead fish. Touched dead fish.

Okay, okay. A couple of dead fish in a lake that's

sixty miles in diameter may not seem like a big deal. Granted, they weren't even big fish. Just little two-inch fish. I have no idea what kind of fish they were. When I was soaping up in the shower I mulled over whether I should try to scoop up a dead fish and have it analyzed. I nixed that idea when I couldn't think what to do with a dead fish. Look up "fish analysis" in the yellow pages? Google "What killed this fish?"

"We don't even know if there are chemicals in the water," Lily said, moving a blow dryer around Mango. He may not have liked the bath portion of his treatment, but he was pretty happy about the blow dryer. Or maybe he just liked having two girls spend so much time combing and cooing and cuddling him.

"Something's in the water. You saw it, too. The stuff that Marcus's parents put in this morning looked like laundry detergent," I said.

"Maybe it was Tide or Cheer or something," Lily said. "Wouldn't that just clean the water? Tidy it up? Cheer the fish?"

"Oh, come on! Where were you in fourth grade? People can't put detergents and chemicals in the water. It kills things. Maybe even kills fish. Remember when we had to write about that guy in north Seattle who cleaned his driveway with that solvent? The chemicals from his cleaner ran down his driveway, down the hill, and into Lake Washington. He got a huge fine for polluting the water."

"Yeah, I remember," Lily grudgingly agreed.

"And remember when we were in third grade and our field trip to Hood Canal had to be canceled?"

"That was a bummer."

"It was a bigger bummer for the fish that lived there. It was hypoxia, when there isn't much oxygen in the water and it makes these dead zones where deep-water fish can't survive," I said, impressed with my ability to recall the word "hypoxia." Apparently I'd suitably impressed Lily, too.

"I can't believe you remember that. All I remember is that we went to the Children's Museum for about the sixtieth time instead of getting to go to the beach," Lily said.

"Did you hear something?" I asked. Lily turned off the hair dryer. An impatient knocking came at the door.

"Who's there?" I called. It seems kind of stupid to call out like that. It doesn't really protect you from danger. If an ax murderer is on the other side, he isn't exactly going to say, "It's an ax murderer."

"Marcus Dartmouth, director, *Dockside Blues*."

Interesting.

I assumed I'd have my mother's permission to open the door for Alice's nephew, who just happened to be a television producer and director. I opened the door but didn't invite him in. Mom would have my hide if I invited someone into the house when she wasn't there, even if it was a Hollywood director.

"We're going ahead with the shot of you and that dog in the water. I need your parent or legal guardian's permission for you to be on *Dockside Blues*," he said.

Wait a second. Who did this guy think he was, assuming I'd want to be in a primetime television show?

Wait just another second. Who did I think I was, waiting even a second to reply? Oops. Wait again. Lily was the actress. She was the one who wanted a role on this show. How could I be on *Dockside Blues* without my best friend?

"We'll need your friend as well, since she's in the shot where Monica gets out of the water," Marcus said.

Whew, I thought to myself. "Her name is Lily Shannon and my name is Hannah West, and we'll have to talk with our parents to see if we can get their permission. We'll get back to you."

I closed the door.

Lily and I did a silent happy dance, jumping up and down, and mouthing, We're going to be on TV! We're going to be on TV!

Mango was not so silent.

CHAPTER 14

IF I THOUGHT WATCHING A TV SHOW BEING SHOT WAS A BIG SNORE, I HAD no idea that having a teensy tiny part on a cable TV series could possibly be so dull either. Here's my advice to actors and actresses everywhere: Bring something to read on the set. Two minutes of glory in front of the camera means eight hours of agony, just sitting around waiting for something to happen.

The worst part was that because my big entrance was done soaking wet, I had to stay soaking wet. I refused to get in the lake water again, so they kept hosing me off. Chet, a guy on the crew, rigged the hose up through a houseboat's outdoor utility sink so at least the water was lukewarm. Still, I was sick of being wet.

Lily and I had called our parents the second we got the big TV news. All responsible adults had agreed that we could participate, and they'd talked to Celeste, the P.A., to verify that they'd sign all the necessary paperwork at the end of the day when they came to Portage Bay.

Lily's dad, Dan, returned from his hundred-mile bike ride and started to fill out her permission forms.

"I really should have Lily's agent look this over first," he said, handing a stack of papers over to Celeste. Lily and I both groaned at Dan's lame attempt to be funny.

We were each getting a hundred dollars a day. Sounds pretty good, until we found out that tomorrow was going to be our last day. Oh well. That's still two hundred dollars of easy money. That is, if you think it's easy to sit around and be bored and then be wet. Mango was getting the same fee. I volunteered to accept his payment, since I think of myself as his professional handler as well as his walker and his poop picker-upper. But Mom had Celeste take down all of Jake's information for payment.

"You're going to get some mighty nice raw bones there, boy," I said to Mango, giving him a belly rub.

Evenings on the houseboat were wonderful. Everything smelled fresh and clean. It was quiet, especially compared to the way it was during the day with a TV crew on this dock. And with a dog barking. And with an actress screaming.

I looked over the edge of the dock into the water. It didn't *look* dirty or contaminated. It didn't *smell* toxic.

"Let's take out the double kayak," Mom said. She was home after a long shift at Wired Café. She'd taken Mango out for a short jog and was now showered and changed into shorts and a T-shirt.

"I don't know if we should be in the water," I said.

Mom has always said that a big imagination was one of the best things you could have. Would I sound crazy if I told her that I kept seeing people dressed in black scurrying around with buckets and bottles? I don't know if I'd believe myself if I heard that one. But she's my mom, so she kind of has to put up with me. I decided to tell her everything I'd seen in the past few days.

"I'm not sure what Alice has to do with any of this, but remember how we saw her at the island nation of Tui Tui with those glass jars?" I asked.

Mom nodded.

"Well I've seen her a few more times. At first I thought she was putting something into the water, but now I think she's getting samples."

"What do you think she does with those samples?" Mom asked.

"I don't know. But I'm thinking we should get some samples of our own," I said.

"And what do you plan to do with those water samples? Test them in our basement science laboratory?" Mom asked. Geesh. She sounded like an echo of Lily, making fun of me.

"Look over there," I said, pointing across the bay toward the University of Washington. "I bet there's some research lab there that would help us. All we'd need to do is collect the samples."

"Okay. But now you've got me freaked out about what might be in the water. I hope Alice was overreacting. We should be okay in a kayak. But just in case, let's be extra careful when we gather the water samples," Mom said. She grabbed some Nalgene water bottles from REI and tossed them into a backpack. She tossed in some bagels, grapes, cheese, and bottled water as well. "We might as well have a picnic while we're out there," she said. "We can hose off the kayak as soon as we get back. Just in case."

Just in case there really was something deadly in the water? I was counting on Mom to be calm and rational. She was supposed to balance out my overactive imagination. Suddenly the idea of a picnic on a potential cesspool of water didn't sound too appetizing.

I tossed my essential supplies into a backpack, too. Camera, film, Sharpie, paper, pencil. Everything an amateur sleuth/photographer needs.

This time I let Mom paddle shotgun. In other words, she got the front seat. She pulls harder than I do, anyway, so it's easier to let her be in the lead and do the steering. Otherwise she's a total backseat paddler, telling me to stroke more on the starboard or port side, which doesn't really help get us anywhere any faster because I have to stop and think: starboard means right, port means left. Being in the rear seat makes it easier for me to slack off and take photos, too.

As we reached the middle of the lake and stopped paddling, Mom said, "Now there's a yacht." We were resting and letting the wake in the water bob us along. It felt like a mini-roller-coaster ride every time a big motorboat went by. I followed her gaze right to the *Clean Sweep.* "It's going pretty fast through here, don't you think?"

"Mom, look at the name on that boat," I said. She squinted and took her sunglasses off, but I could tell she couldn't see it clearly. I handed her my camera with the zoom lens. "Oh, my. Is that Marcus's parents' boat? The one you were telling me about?"

"Yep. But remember, it's a *yacht*, not a boat."

"Look, they're slowing down. They must have real-ized they were speeding." Mom handed the camera back to me. I focused on Timothy, who was wearing his captain's hat. Stella was dropping an anchor. They were close to their yacht club, yet they'd put an anchor down instead of taking their boat into the moorage. I was about to put the camera down when I saw Timothy carry a big white bucket to the side where Stella was. She began scooping something out of the bucket and putting it in the water. I snapped a bunch of pictures, even though I had no idea what I was photographing.

Timothy brought up the anchor, and Stella started the motor. The *Clean Sweep* puttered into the covered docks at the Emerald City Yacht Club.

"Can you keep your eye on the exact spot where they just were?" I asked Mom.

"Got it," she said. "Let's go."

We paddled to the area where the *Clean Sweep* had just been.

"Okay, hand me one of the bottles and I'll get a sample," Mom said.

"Hand you a bottle? What do you mean? You packed the backpack. You have the bottles."

"I saw you bring a backpack," Mom said.

"Right. I brought *my* backpack. You had the other one."

We were silent for a couple of moments. "So, I guess that means that neither one of us has the jars to get a sample. I guess there's only one thing to do." I took out my water bottle.

"Hannah! Don't empty your water right here. If there's anything to be found in a water sample, you might interfere with it," Mom said.

"I wasn't going to," I said. And then I chugged an entire bottle of water.

It was kind of tricky to get a water sample without touching the lake water. In fact, I did get my fingers a little wet.

"Just don't rub your eyes or touch your face," Mom said. That, of course, made my eyes itch like crazy and I had a terrible urge to rub my eyes and my nose and every other inch of my face. "Let's get home as fast as possible."

As soon as we got home, I sat in bed with Mango and the laptop. I went to the Department of Fisheries Web site at the University of Washington and started reading about what different researchers were working on. I had no idea that studying fish could be so incredibly complicated. "Hmmm . . . she sounds promising," I told Mango. Alpha B. Cowlitz got my attention first because of her name, but her university Web site said she was particularly interested in urban water-ways and taking action to preserve healthy water quality. Best yet, she had a link from her Web site to a personal Web site that talked about how she loved to kayak and row. In fact, she rowed crew with a recre-ational team from the university boathouse, conve-niently located just across the bay from our dock.

Isn't e-mail great? I get kind of sick of hearing adults complain about how much e-mail they get and how much time it takes. Me? I love it. Especially when I can make myself "look" older through an e-mail message. It gives me extra confidence that I wouldn't have on the phone. No one can tell that I'm just a seventh grader. The trick, you see, is to restrain your-self from trying to sound too much like an adult, which can end up sounding stuffy if you're not careful. Anything too formal or distinguished can be a dead giveaway that you're up to something. Simple and straightforward is what I find works best when you want answers from an adult:

Dear Ms. Cowlitz,

I'm a resident on Portage Bay in Lake Washington near your university. I see that you're interested in urban water issues and I'm wondering if I could enlist your help. I would like to have our water tested. Just a simple test so I won't worry about my puppy, Mango, going for an occasional swim.

Perhaps this will tie in with your own research in some way.

Thank you.

Sincerely,
Hannah J. West

You might notice that I slipped Mango into my query as well. People are suckers for dogs, especially puppies, and I'm sure Mango's youthful personality makes him appear puppylike. I included his name for extra authenticity.

I was Googling "Monica Heathcliff" and "Marcus Dartmouth, director" when my Mac Mail dinged, letting me know I had a new message.

From: Alpha B. Cowlitz

Dear Ms. West,
I'm particularly interested in local urban water quality. I'll be in the lab each day this week from 9 a.m. to 5 p.m. You can call or e-mail me there, or stop by.

She left her lab address and a link to a university map that showed the lab's location on the campus. I whipped out my bus schedules for the number 25 and number 66. Bummer! I'd completely forgotten that I had a television shoot the next day. Oh, it's so hard being a TV star. I had an eight o'clock "call" in the morning. Saving Portage Bay would just have to be put on hold while I pursued my selfish dreams of stardom.

Mango did his tap-dancing routine that meant he had to go relieve himself one last time before turning in for the night.

"Mom, I'm going to the sidewalk to let Mango pee," I called up to the sleeping loft.

"Take a flashlight and come right back," she said.

I'm not easily spooked, but the stillness of the air at night and the lapping sound of the water was kind of creepy. I walked quickly to the little patch of grass that Mango liked to use as his personal bathroom. Luckily, he only peed, and I didn't have to pick anything up. We headed back out the dock when I saw a lantern bobbing out on the water. I could just barely see the outline of a woman in a kayak. I tried to relax my eyes, just like we talk about in art and photography so that I could take in everything a bit easier. See things I hadn't seen before. Well, I saw something I hadn't seen before all right. Alice Campbell was out on the water in a kayak. I could tell from her movements that she was scooping water into bottles and then stowing them in her kayak. I dashed inside and grabbed the camera.

When I came out, I looked through the camera lens and realized it wasn't Alice after all. It was Estie. Out alone in the dark on the water. I took a photograph.

Oops.

Unfortunately, the flash went off. The bright light on a dark night startled me. But not as much as it startled Estie. She screamed as she fell into the water.

I wanted to run back inside and turn off all the lights and pretend that it wasn't me. But what if she was as big of a spaz as Monica Heathcliff in the water?

"Are you okay?" I called out over the water. My voice sounded high and screechy as it interrupted the night.

"I'll be fine," Estie said. She wasn't actually that far out, I realized. It had seemed farther when I'd first spotted her.

"Who's in the water? Does someone need help?" Alice came out of her cottage wearing a fluffy white bathrobe and flip-flops. She looked out at the water. "Oh, dear. Is that you, Estie? Bring the boat back in and come to my house. You can have a nice warm shower, and I'll make you a cup of tea."

Alice turned to me. "Estie asked to borrow my kayak for a little moonlight paddle. I should have asked more about her skills," she said with a slight chuckle.

"I think something startled her out there," I said. Yeah, and that "something" was me and my stupid camera flash.

"I'm sure everything is fine. Good night, Hannah," Alice said. I gratefully went inside, happy that Mango and I were both dry for a change.

But even with Alice's reassurances, I couldn't help but wonder what Estie had really been doing out kayaking in the dark.

CHAPTER 15

MONDAY MORNING I WAS UP EARLY, HAD THE DOG WALKED, MY CAP'N CRUNCH eaten, and my reading material ready when I went to my high-powered television job.

I looked out the window and saw Lily walking out onto the dock. I grabbed my camera off the table—just in case I had a chance to take some pictures of the actors—and headed out the door. "Whew! What a long commute," I announced as I walked out of our houseboat and onto the set.

"Funny," Lily said. "Do I look okay? Do you know what we're going to do today?"

I held up a book called *Lulu Dark Can See Through Walls* in response. I had a feeling I knew exactly what I was going to be doing today: sitting around and reading. And, might I add, making one hundred dollars for my efforts.

"Girls, I'm glad you're here and ready to go," Celeste

said. She checked something off a list on her clipboard. "We're going to have to shoot around Monica's scenes today."

"Why?" I asked. I had to keep myself from asking if she was afraid of the fish-killing toxic water.

"She had to fly back to L.A. unexpectedly," Celeste said.

"A hair emergency?" I asked. Lily kicked me. "Ow!"

"We have someone to stand in for Monica, and we should be okay as long as we don't get too close," Celeste said.

"Wow. Monica has a double. Who is it?" Lily asked.

"I'd be the last to know. Remember, I'm just the lowly production assistant," Celeste said.

"Tsk, tsk. Don't talk that way." Marcus Dartmouth came up behind Celeste, who immediately turned beet-colored from head to neck. "The P.A. is the most essential person on the crew. Not counting the actors. Or the director. Or the producers, makeup people, writers, continuity director, grips, and camera crew." If he intended a compliment, he certainly failed, as he'd named just about everybody he could possibly name, except for the lunch crew. "Oh, and the caterers. Food people are definitely way up there." Marcus turned around and barked orders to the people setting up the scene.

"And here's our stand-in," he announced proudly. A woman who looked remarkably similar to Monica Heathcliff smiled at everyone. There was something really eerie about her. She could pass as Monica II. Yet something was a little off, most notably the obvious wig of stiff blond hair she was wearing. Her smile went to half-mast.

Bingo!

"Could I take a quick picture?" I asked the new actress. I used my supersweet voice and I was trying to look wide-eyed and easily impressed. Lily looked at me, puzzled. Monica II nodded and the full smile returned to her face. I snapped a photo of Estie Bartlett dressed as Monica Heathcliff.

"Pay attention!" Lily elbowed me back to *Dockside Blues*.

"Your jobs are to act natural," Marcus instructed us. "Act like you live here."

I *do* live here, I wanted to say.

"We're taking establishing shots first. We'll set the scene with Seattle, some shots from the water, and then some shots of you doing teenage-type things," he continued.

Teenage-type things? Cool! He thought we were teenagers. I was interested to see how they'd stage "teenage-type things."

"Here, start tossing this Frisbee back and forth," Marcus instructed us.

No problem. Both Lily and I are ultimate Frisbee players, so a little dock tossing was supereasy for us. That is, it was supereasy if we were actually paying attention. But it gets a little dull to have people telling you when to smile and how to toss and which way to look and all that. So much for acting naturally. When Marcus instructed me to throw the Frisbee in a totally lame arm movement, I followed his orders and the disc went right over Lily's head and into the water.

"Mango! No!" I said. It was a halfhearted attempt to get him to stop, because truly, I was hoping the dog would do the dogly thing and chew up the Frisbee. A few gnashes with his teeth and the Frisbee wouldn't be worthy of *Dockside Blues*.

"Wait! Mango, no!" This time I really meant no. Because for Mango to get the Frisbee, he'd have to get in the water. Into the icky, scary, possibly contaminated water.

Splash! I had to admit he looked gorgeous going in.

"Brilliant! Simply brilliant! We have yet another shot with the dog in the water. I love it. So authentic," Marcus was going on and on.

"Mr. Dartmouth, I hope you have enough now,

because we need to get Mango washed off after being in the lake water," I said, using my superpolite voice.

"Good, good. Yes, get him cleaned up and dried off and we'll shoot it all over again. I want to re-create that last scene down to the smallest detail, but we'll need to start with a dry dog."

Was he serious?

"Actually, I need to get Mango clean and keep him clean," I said.

"You can clean him up, but as I outlined to you earlier, we'll need to go through the sequence of him in the water again," Marcus said.

Here's what I wanted to say next: With all due respect, sir, we cannot let this dog submerge in the lake water again because of unknown contaminants—quite possibly caused by your mother and stepfather—currently in the water. Then I'd take Mango and march confidently toward the end of the dock where I'd go into our gorgeous houseboat and slam the door.

Here's what I said: "Um, I'd better talk with his owner before Mango goes swimming in this water anymore. It might not be good for him."

You can see my dilemma. Okay, two dilemmas. The first is that I'm a total wimp when it comes to direct confrontation. The second is that I'm a total wimp, and

I didn't want to get between Mr. Hollywood Hotshot and his Potential Polluter Parents. The only thing I had the guts to stand up for was Mango.

"Fine, fine. I think we have enough. Celeste, take care of these girls. Everyone else, let's break for lunch."

Estie looked completely disappointed that half a day of shooting was over, and she hadn't been in one single scene.

"Come on, Mango," I said to the sopping wet dog. "I think you know the drill." He followed me into the houseboat and into his now familiar bath ritual.

After lunch, Lily, Mango, and I headed up to the bus stop. The Metro bus pulled up right on schedule. I scanned my pass and deposited $1.25 for Mango. "Does your dog need a transfer?" the driver asked, with a smile.

"Sure, thanks."

Lily put her money in. "Her friend needs a transfer, too, please," she said. "It's not fair," she said as she sat down beside me. "Dogs get all the attention."

We got off in the middle of the University of Washington by the Husky Union Building. I waited with Lily until the number 67 came by to take her home. She had to babysit her little brother for the rest of the afternoon. She's not as experienced at riding buses as I am, and I felt kind of protective of her. I wanted to make sure she got on the right one.

As her bus drove away, I pulled out the map I'd printed from the university Web site and headed south through campus to the research building. I started to lead Mango up the steps, and then I spotted the NO DOGS ALLOWED sign hanging on the door. I pulled out my cell phone and called the number Alpha had given me.

"Hello, this is Hannah West. I contacted you about the water in Portage Bay," I said.

"Yes, of course. I'm anxious to meet you," Alpha replied.

"I'm actually right outside of your building, but I have my dog with me. Should I wait for you out here?"

"Wait there and I'll come get you. If you're with me, it won't be any problem to have a dog inside."

A few seconds later a thin woman with long black hair in a ponytail came out. She looked at us and kept looking. She looked again. Mango was, after all, the only dog around.

"Excuse me, are you Hannah?" she asked.

"Yes, I am." I tried to look older than seventh grade. Who was I trying to impress? This woman was wearing a Hello Kitty T-shirt.

"Sorry, I thought you'd be older," she said.

"I thought you would be, too," I countered.

"I'm old enough," she said a little defensively. "I'm twenty-five."

"This is Mango," I said, hoping to get on her good side with my cute dog. "He's the reason I'm worried about the water quality in the lake."

She looked at us again and then sighed and said, "Come inside and we can talk." Mango and I followed her into the brick research building, down a flight of stairs, and through a long hallway painted a garish blend of green and yellow. "I share an office with another graduate student, but he's not here right now." She moved a stack of papers off of a wood chair and gestured for me to sit down.

"I brought a water sample I took yesterday," I said. I took my TalkingRain bottle out of my messenger bag and set it down. I'd used a Sharpie to write the time and date on the bottle. I pulled out a map of Portage Bay and handed it to her, too. "I marked the spot where I got the water. Or at least the general area."

"Why did you choose this particular spot to take a water sample? Is this where your dog likes to swim? It seems pretty far from shore."

"Um, actually, this isn't where he swims. My mom

and I were kayaking last night when we got this sample," I started to explain.

"Why this spot?"

"Well, we saw a suspicious-looking boat in the area, and we wanted to see what they were up to. I thought maybe they were dumping something in the water," I said.

"Or they could be, like you, trying to get water samples to study." Why was this woman challenging me on this? Maybe Alpha B. Cowlitz was not the kind of researcher who wanted to help a kid. Maybe her interest in healthy urban waterways was tied to wealthy urban donors. Maybe she'd thought I was an adult with lots of money, based on where I said I lived. I had only one more trick up my sleeve. Honesty.

"Listen, my mom and I are house-sitting on a houseboat on Portage Bay. I've seen some weird things that make me wonder about the water, including some little dead fish right off our dock. I looked through newspaper archives and couldn't find any stories about anything being dumped in the water. There haven't been any warnings not to swim. But there's definitely something strange going on."

Alpha seemed to relax and get more interested in

my problem. Maybe she could see that I was serious.

"Hannah, you said you live on a houseboat. Can you give me an exact address?"

I gave it to her, and after she wrote it down she went to a tall metal file cabinet and pulled out a file.

"Have you talked to any of your neighbors about this?" she asked.

"No. Not yet."

"Hannah, I won't be able to test your water sample," she said.

Drat! I thought I had her. But she kept talking.

"I'll have to get my own water samples and do it systematically and scientifically. Not that you did anything wrong. You did a great job with the general location and the date and time. But I'll need more specific information."

"Does this mean you'll help me?" I asked.

"I will. This ties directly into my own research project."

"Do you think that yachts might be involved in polluting the water?" I asked.

"I can't tell yet. I can tell you that it's not just a case of gasoline-powered engines and their exhaust causing the trouble. I do have a hunch that power boats are involved, however," she said.

Boats involved, but not because of their engines? I wished she would tell me more, but she insisted she needed to do some tests first.

"And before we take this any further, there's someone else I think you should talk to," Alpha said.

"Who?"

"Alice Campbell."

CHAPTER 16

MANGO AND I GOT BACK TO THE DOCK WHILE THE CREW WAS STILL filming. I plopped down on the sidewalk by the mail-boxes and tried to figure out what to do.

"Aren't they done yet?" Alice asked as she wandered back toward the dock. Just the person I wanted to see. Especially since Alpha had just mentioned her.

"Nope. They're still here," I said, stating the obvious.

"Well, I was planning on going home, but luckily I'm dressed for my daily walk," Alice said, gesturing at her black tracksuit. Mango barked when he heard the word "walk."

"That's right, I love to walk, don't I?" Alice said, obviously enjoying egging Mango on. "I walk four miles every day." He barked each time she said "walk." Alice laughed each time he barked. "I think Mango would like to accompany me," she said. "Would you like to join us?"

Of course I wanted to go on a walk with her. This was the perfect chance to ask her what she'd been up to. I was going to be smooth, though, and follow her lead about the right time to start asking questions. I'd warm her up. Get her talking about other things. I'd let her set the pace.

Alice also set the pace for walking. And what a pace. Yowza. You can never tell how hilly a place is until you're on your feet or pedaling a bike. We had maybe two blocks of flat streets, and then we went up a supersteep hill that had ridges in the sidewalk to keep people from toppling over when they came down. Alice walked fast—and I do mean fast. It was hot, and I was hot. "Do you always walk this fast? For the whole four miles?" I asked.

"We'll only go a couple miles this afternoon," she said. "But to answer your question, I like to walk fast. I ran until I was fifty-three. Arthritis in my knee slowed me down to a walk."

"I wouldn't call this slow," I said, huffing as we entered a dense, shady forest. "Wow. Where are we? Is this some kind of park?"

"Not just any park. This is a historical section of Seattle," Alice began. "Imagine this at the turn of the century. Make that the turn of the twentieth century, more than one hundred years ago. Bicycles and horses and buggies were favored forms of transportation then. This park was designed as a bicycle boulevard linking downtown and Capitol Hill to the shores of Lake Washington. At one time these pathways were filled with cyclists on their way to picnics or to work."

I could totally imagine it. Wide paths meandered up the steep face of Capitol Hill, with lush forest growth on each side of the paths, making it shady and cool. I suppose the trees could even protect bicyclists from the rain. They were that thick.

"I can't imagine riding up this without a twenty-four-speed bike," I said.

"You'd have to stand up on your pedals and work your muscles hard," Alice said. "Of course, there's no shame in getting off a bike and walking it uphill either. But you'd want to stay on your bike for the downhill ride. It must have been exhilarating."

"This is so cool! And it must smell really good, too," I said. Mango was sniffing around like crazy.

"I like to bring people here so that others will realize what a treasure we have in this park. We still have fifty-one acres here."

"Do you think we're in danger of losing it?" I asked, feeling a bit panicky.

"Oh, there's always that chance. This is prime real estate. But it's also an important part of Seattle's history. Part of the city's legacy. Some of our most gorgeous parks, including this one, are thanks to the Olmsted brothers, sons of the man who designed New York's Central Park."

I was quiet for a while, mostly because we were going up such a steep incline.

"Whoa! What's that?" I asked as we approached a tall brick structure. It towered over the trees ahead of us. "I had no idea a place like this existed in Seattle."

"It's now the Seattle Hebrew Academy. It was first built in 1916 as a convent. It was situated here, by Interlaken Park, to be far from the wicked ways of Seattle proper. It's a gorgeous building, isn't it?"

"I wonder if the nuns liked living there," I said.

She stopped walking and looked directly at me.

"I wonder if you're wondering about something else," Alice said.

"Well, actually, I am."

"I told you earlier, if you're wondering about something, all you have to do is ask," she said.

Here goes: "Who are you trying to protect?" I blurted out.

CHAPTER 17

ALICE STARTED WALKING AGAIN WITHOUT ANSWERING ME. SHE SEEMED intent on watching the pathway as we wound our way back down the steep hills of Interlaken Park.

"It's Marcus, isn't it?" I prodded.

Still no answer.

"Marcus's parents are doing something weird to the water. And you're trying to cover for them. You're not just covering for them, though. You want to make sure that Marcus isn't hurt by what they're doing."

"No, that isn't it," Alice said. She sounded much older and more tired than when she was giving me the historic tour of the park.

"So you're not trying to protect him?" We were going downhill, heading back toward Lake Washington and the Portage Bay dock.

"It's complicated, Hannah."

"If something is in the water that can kill fish, we

have to stop it, no matter how complicated it is," I said. I couldn't help it when an argumentative tone crept into my voice. But this was big-time stuff.

"I agree with you completely, Hannah. We need to stop whatever is going on," Alice said.

"Then let's stop it!" I said adamantly. "Mom has a friend at KOMO TV. We can call her once we get Alpha's water test results. We can go to the city council and the newspapers."

"You know Alpha?" Alice asked. She'd looked so serious just moments ago, but now she smiled. "My, you do get around, don't you?"

"The thing is, I still don't know what's going into the water or why it's going in," I said.

"There's still a lot I need to sort out," Alice said. Then she went into silent mode for the rest of our walk back to the dock.

Alpha Cowlitz, the university researcher, was just getting off the bus when Alice and I got back down to Boyer Avenue.

"Alpha!" Alice called. "It's wonderful to see you. Although I can't say I'm surprised. We were just talking about you."

Alice invited Alpha and me into her cottage. She put

a bowl of water down for Mango, who lapped it up sloppily and then lay down on the cool kitchen floor.

"Alice, I told Hannah that I need to do systematic testing to get any reliable readings on the water quality here," Alpha began. "But I couldn't resist doing some preliminary tests on the samples you gave me already."

"Before you go any further, I want to give Hannah a bit of background," Alice said. "Residents on this part of Lake Washington, here in Portage Bay, have a long history of fighting for clean water."

Here we go again, I thought. I might as well put all questions on hold until Alice gave me another Seattle history lesson.

"It's almost impossible to believe," Alice continued, "but back in the 1970s the city of Seattle used to actually dump raw sewage into the water here."

"Gross!" I couldn't help interrupting.

"Yes, it's gross. And unconscionable. One would think that we would have learned by now to be careful what we put in the water. Still, there are people living in big houses who use toxic chemicals to clean their driveways and patios, and then hose off the cleaner, and the runoff then gets into our lakes and streams.

"In the early summer I noticed that some of the plant life in the lake seemed to be particularly robust. We had an unusually dry and warm spring, as you might recall. When I was kayaking, I'd often find my paddle hitting a plant or bringing up plant material. Then, about two weeks ago, I realized that I'd had several kayak sessions without encountering any aquatic plants. And of course that ridiculous actress saw those dead fish."

"I'm not surprised that the aquatic plants have receded," Alpha said. "I've noticed the same thing when I'm rowing from the Pocock Center at the university. It makes perfect sense with what I found in the water samples."

Alice and I looked at Alpha, waiting for her to continue. "What did you find?" Alice prodded.

"Herbicides."

"Herbicides?" I asked.

Alpha explained that certain types of plants in the lake could actually take root on boats—a fact that didn't go over so well in the yachting community.

It all started to make sense. They weren't trying to kill fish. They were trying to kill plants.

Lily's lame joke from earlier in the week echoed in my head. She'd said: "Maybe it was Tide or Cheer or something. Wouldn't that just clean the water? Tidy it up?" In a twisted way, she was right. Because someone had the extra-twisted idea of dumping herbicides in the water so that those big expensive boats would be cleaner.

CHAPTER 18

"I GOT THESE DEVELOPED FOR YOU," MOM SAID, HANDING ME THREE packages of developed film. "They're on this CD, too."

"You're the best mom ever!" I said, snatching the envelopes from her.

"Does that mean you want to come with me tonight when I go back downtown to review an art opening?" she asked.

"Actually, it doesn't mean that at all. But you're still the best. As long as you let me stay home and go kayaking tonight," I said. "I need to get some more photos to fill in a couple of gaps here." I spread my new black-and-white photos across the kitchen table, organizing them as I went. I had the pictures of Stella and Timothy on the *Clean Sweep*, the shot of Estie night kayaking, and many more. As I looked through them, more and more pieces of the puzzle started to come into focus, so to speak. But there were still a few things I didn't fully understand.

"If we get up early, you and I can kayak tomorrow morning," Mom said. "But you are not allowed to take Jake's boat out alone. I'm glad he has a double kayak so you won't be tempted," she added. "But even if he had a single, you are not to go out alone. I repeat: You, Hannah West, may not go out on the water alone tonight. Or at any other time. Understood?"

"I understand you perfectly," I said. I stormed off to my temporary bedroom with Mango right at my heels. It's hard to sulk properly with an adorable labradoodle, so I curled up on the bed with the pooch and did some online research about aquatic plants. After Mom left, I got my camera out anyway and headed outside. Through the telephoto lens I saw a woman with long blond hair emptying a garbage pail into the water from a small motorboat.

Click. Refocus. Advance the film. *Click.* This was great stuff! It might not have anything to do with herbicides, but it reminded me of those nuts in the 1970s dumping sewage into the lake. This woman was emptying an entire garbage can! *Click.* There's no way she could have heard me—I was a hundred yards away—but she looked up and directly into the camera.

Monica Heathcliff! I could see the headline right above my photo: "Famous Hollywood Actress Litters in Lake— photos by Hannah West." I zoomed in again and caught her mouth in a position that I recognized. It wasn't Monica after all. It was Estie. Just like that, my dreams of selling my photos to *Hollywood Star* evaporated.

I kept snapping anyway.

Splash. I took my eye from the viewfinder and saw Alice Campbell taking her kayak in the water. The usually graceful Alice wasn't typically a splasher, but she was definitely in a hurry. She stroked strong and deep, making incredible speed for a human-powered boat.

She was heading right for where I'd seen Monica Heathcliff. Or was she heading to the boat nearby? I looked through the camera again.

The *Clean Sweep* was crisply framed in my viewfinder.

I slung the camera strap around my neck and clumsily got Jake's kayak down and into the water. I looked around, hoping one of the other neighbors might be around. I was itching to get on the water, but I'd promised I wouldn't go out alone.

Turns out someone else was itching to get on the water.

Thud. I turned back to the kayak.

"Mango! How did you get in there, boy?"

Sitting in the backseat of Jake Heard's double kayak was his dog. He obviously wanted to go for a ride . . . and that meant I wouldn't be alone. Maybe this was exactly why Jake had a double in the first place.

"Okay, Mango, you're on!" I grabbed a paddle and eased quickly into the front spot of the kayak. My strokes weren't as deep or as quick as Alice's were, but I made amazingly good time out into the water. Monica Heathcliff's boat must have motored off, but Alice was almost out to the *Clean Sweep.* I had a great view, so I pulled to a stop and fiddled with the camera until Alice, Timothy, and Stella were all in view. Stella leaned over the side of the boat, talking earnestly to Alice below. Alice began raising out of the kayak, as if she were going to pull herself onto the yacht. Stella leaned over further and—

"Alice!" I screamed.

But she was already in the water. I'd captured her tumble into the water on film. I thought Stella had pushed her, and I was pretty sure I'd have a photo to prove it. But there was no more time for photos. I started stroking as fast as I could toward the *Clean Sweep,* with Mango announcing our arrival in a series of quick barks.

"Alice!" I called out. She was now up in the boat, and Timothy had draped a blanket around her wet shoulders. Stella was crying. And Alice was crying.

"I'm so sorry," Alice said.

"No, no, I'm so sorry that we suspected you," Stella said.

Huh?

CHAPTER 19

FIFTEEN MINUTES LATER, MANGO AND I WERE ABOARD A GIGANTIC YACHT pleasure cruising toward the Emerald City Yacht Club. Stella and Timothy had rushed Alice back to her houseboat so she could take a shower. While she got thoroughly clean, Stella had called Maggie on her cell phone to ask if I could accompany Alice as their guests to the yacht club.

I was trying to be patient, but there was still so much to know. Still, this was my first time on a pleasure-cruising yacht, and I was determined to enjoy the ride.

"This is the life, isn't it, boy?" I said. Mango licked my face and then stretched his head over the side of the boat, just like a dog does in a car when the windows are down.

"I didn't completely suspect you, Alice," Stella was saying when I joined everyone inside the yacht. And

I do mean "yacht." This thing was like a house with a motor. I wanted to snoop around and see what was downstairs, but the conversation up above was just too good to miss. "It's just that I know you'd do anything to protect Marcus. You were always so special to him, and I know you adore him, too." Stella and Alice hugged, and Timothy stood by with a big smile on his face.

"If you two aren't dumping herbicides in the water, who is?" I asked.

Timothy's smile instantly disappeared. "Why on earth would you think that Stella and I would put something toxic into the water?" he demanded.

"Um, well," I stammered. "You see, I had this theory going . . . "

"Let's hear this theory," Timothy said.

No way was I going to tell him what I was thinking. But then his smile returned, and it seemed like a genuine, kind smile.

"You won't hurt our feelings, Hannah. I just really want to know."

"Um, you see, I first thought that it was something emitted from the engine or the fuel used in motorboats. But that wasn't it. But I couldn't get the name of your boat out of my head."

"The *Clean Sweep*?" Stella asked.

"Yeah. *Clean Sweep*. I had a feeling you both liked your boat to be superclean. And maybe that's why you named it the *Clean Sweep*," I said.

"I do like a clean ship," Timothy said.

"But that's not the reason for the name," Stella added.

"I was just guessing. Alice said something about how her paddle kept getting caught in the plants growing in the lake. I thought maybe somehow the plants were interfering with your boat, too. I mean, your yacht."

"That's a pretty good theory," Timothy said.

"But it turns out to be wrong," Stella added.

"I can tell you about the name *Clean Sweep*," Alice said. "I bet Alpha could have guessed it as well. Timothy was a rower in college."

"We made a clean sweep my senior year, taking the national championship from Harvard," Timothy said.

"Did you say something back there about Alpha?" Stella asked. "Such a beautiful but unusual name. Timothy, isn't that the name of the woman we met at Stephen's lab?"

"Who's Stephen?" Alice and I both asked at the same time.

"He's a graduate student over at the university. He

developed the herbicide neutralizer we were testing," Timothy said.

"The what?" Alice and I asked in unison again.

"We're trying to counteract the effects of the chemicals that are attacking the aquatic plant life. We were hoping for an easy fix, but we had no idea that the herbicides would be toxic enough to kill fish as well. The problem is a lot bigger than we first thought," Stella said.

"Why didn't you try to find and stop the polluter instead of covering it up?" I asked. But no one said anything. I wondered if they were afraid to answer. Maybe they didn't want to say that Marcus was the one they suspected. I could tell that Alice didn't want to say that Marcus, her own nephew, was the one she suspected (although it had already come out that Alice suspected Marcus's loving parents of helping him with the scheme). None of the adults wanted to say it, so no one said anything for a while.

"I don't think it was Marcus," I said, interrupting the silence. They all looked at me but were still silent. "Really. I don't think he's behind this. Have you ever asked him?"

They shook their heads.

"By this time tomorrow, I think I can prove who was

behind it," I said with a bit more confidence than I actually felt. The adults didn't look as if they had much confidence in me either.

"Alice, does the Floating Home Association have meetings?" I asked.

"Yes, of course. We have one the day after tomorrow," she said. "It's at my house."

"Do you think you could have it somewhere else instead?" I asked. "That is, of course, if the yacht club would let us."

CHAPTER 20

IT TURNED OUT THAT STELLA DARTMOUTH WAS A VICE PRESIDENT OF THE yacht club, in line to be commodore next year. Scheduling a meeting at the yacht club was no problem when a VP makes the call.

I made sure that Alpha and Stephen, the other researcher, could come to the meeting. Stella invited Marcus. Alice enticed everyone on our dock—plus Lily—to come by offering a free dinner at the yacht club after the meeting. People who had lived near the yacht club for years said they'd never actually been invited inside. Mom called her friend Mary Perez at KOMO TV. If things didn't play out the way I thought they would, Mary could still do a feature story about the Floating Home Association.

"You can add houseboats to the list of stories that people can't resist," Mary said. "Other parts of the country can count only on cute kids and puppies to lure in viewers no matter what. In Seattle, we have kids, puppies, and houseboats."

"Look! It's Monica Heathcliff!" someone said. A woman with blond hair entered the lobby of the Emerald City Yacht Club, creating quite a stir.

"Can't they tell it isn't Monica?" I asked Lily. "That hair color is so obviously fake."

Lily looked at me in disbelief. "And you thought that the real Monica had natural-looking hair? If we hadn't met Monica, if we'd seen her only on TV and in *People* magazine, I bet we'd think this was the real thing."

"Oh, I think we could see through to Estie Bartlett," I said.

"Doubt it," Lily said in a singsong voice.

"Girls, the meeting is about to begin," Alice said.

"Are you nervous?" I asked.

"Not about the meeting. Not even about the TV camera," Alice said. "But I am a bit nervous about the lines you've given me."

"I bet the magic of being around *Dockside Blues* will make you an Emmy Award–winning actress in your own right," Lily said.

"I hope you're right," Alice said. She went up to the front of the room to begin the meeting.

"Before we go through our business agenda, I'd like

to introduce a few special guests and make an exciting announcement," Alice said to the group of about thirty people gathered in a meeting room called the Captain's Room. She introduced Alpha Cowlitz and Stephen Vargas as two "bright young researchers committed to the environment and healthy water." She introduced Stella and Timothy Dartmouth as "our gracious hosts today, who are eager for Emerald City Yacht Club to become more involved in our neighborhood."

"And now I'd like to introduce our special guest, Monica Heathcliff," Alice said. Everyone clapped enthusiastically. Estie was caught off guard at this announcement, but by the time the camera had turned toward her and the applause started, she was tossing her hair and acting as confident as if she really were a Hollywood star.

"Monica is suffering from a bit of voice strain today," Alice looked pointedly at Estie, who obligingly touched her neck as if she might have a sore throat. "She's asked me to go ahead and make her exciting announcement." Alice paused for drama before continuing, "I feel so privileged to tell you that Monica Heathcliff and her sister, Estie Bartlett, have begun a Portage Bay Stewardship program to ensure that we have healthy, clean water for decades to come." There was spontaneous applause. The next moment was a true test of Estie's acting abilities. She looked stunned. Confused. Angry. And then, magically, she smiled radiantly and nodded. Again her fingers went to her neck and her supposed sore throat. "In addition, these two environmentally conscious sisters will be working with the Emerald City Yacht Club and boating groups to spread the word about healthy water and safe boating." Alice continued with a list of all the commitments we'd dreamed up for Estie.

I passed a small notebook with photos to Estie.

"What's this?" she asked out of the side of her mouth.

"It's just a little motivation to help you remember why you are so committed to the cleanup effort here on Portage Bay," I said. Estie grimaced as she turned the pages. "Nice close-up," I added as she got to the photos I'd taken of her pouring something into the water off the dock, pouring something into the water from a kayak. "You can imagine how excited I was to find such a famous actress in the background of some of my shots."

Estie just nodded and continued smiling.

I'd managed to zoom in pretty well on Estie's face in those shots. What I hadn't expected was the bonus of finding her in eight of my other pictures. I'd taken the digital files and enlarged them in Photoshop. That's when I noticed a woman with long blond hair in a boat near the subject of my shots. I considered them extra insurance. Estie might possibly claim that she was just helping investigate water problems by gathering water samples. However, these shots clearly—or at least somewhat clearly—showed her pouring a powdered substance into the water.

Sitting through the business meeting of the Floating Home Association wasn't exactly exciting, but I bet it was even tougher for Estie to sit through it all.

CHAPTER 21

"This kind of litter patrol totally rocks!" Lily said, moving from side to side so that our double kayak was actually rocking.

"Stop it or I'm going to have to send you to shore patrol," I said. Our job was to paddle around and look for any floating soda cups, beer cans, plastic bags, and other trash that might have landed on the water.

Monica Heathcliff—the real Monica Heathcliff—and her brown-haired sister Estie Bartlett were picking up trash on the shore and surrounding neighborhood. About twenty other people had shown up as part of the Portage Bay Stewardship Cleanup Day.

It turns out I really did have photos of a famous actress littering. I spent more time in Photoshop cleaning up and enlarging and found that there were actually two different women in the backgrounds of some of the photos. Five of the photos had Estie, but three had Monica, who, it turns out, had enlisted Estie's help. In return, Monica promised to help her sister get a role in a television show.

"Why would Monica be interested in polluting water up here?" Marcus had asked me at dinner the night we committed Monica and Estie to being environmental advocates.

"I wasn't sure at first, either," I admitted. "I found a photo of her in *People* with a guy who is supposedly in real estate in Seattle, according to the caption."

"That would be Harrison Donegal," Marcus said. "They're engaged."

"Harrison? Is that the fellow who recently joined the yacht club?" Timothy asked his wife.

"I believe it is," I answered for Stella. "I found out that he owns a thirty-two-foot boat but has just ordered a new sixty-footer that's going to be delivered next month."

"He wanted the plants cut back for his new luxury yacht," Alice said.

"Yep," I said.

Harrison Donegal wasn't on hand to pick up trash. I'd have to find some other way to make sure that he paid for what he did. Alice and her neighbors assured me they could think up some sort of charitable task for him to take on.

"I still don't get why you guys didn't just expose the people who were dumping the herbicides," Lily said.

"Alice tried contacting someone to take action or to charge them with polluting or illegal dumping. Everything is a big mess because there are at least five towns that border the lake plus the Archipelago of Tui Tui, and they're not sure which one of them will press charges. It could take months—or longer—for them to get it all straightened out," I said.

"That's gross. They're getting off way too easy," Lily said.

"The story isn't over. Look, there's Mary!" I waved to Mom's friend the television reporter, who had a camera woman with her today. She was getting some footage to round out her story about illegal dumping. Alpha had already given her preliminary water test results to Mary. I didn't know if my photos would play any role or not, but at least I had them in case anyone decided to charge Estie and Monica with some kind of crime.

"Hey, Hannah," said Polly Summers, Mom's friend who had just paddled up in a kayak with her husband, Tom. As avid kayakers, they were helping to clean up the bay as well. "I just told your mom that I got a lead on someone in Fremont who needs a live-in dogsitter while she goes to Hong Kong for a business trip. You could be living in—"

"The Center of the Universe!" I finished for her. Fremont is this funky, artsy Seattle neighborhood that decided to name itself the Center of the Universe. If I could walk on water living in Portage Bay, who's to say I can't journey to the Center of the Universe?

Don't miss the next exciting Hannah West adventure,
HANNAH WEST IN THE CENTER OF THE UNIVERSE

THE LOCATION: Funky Fremont—known to residents as the Center of the Universe

THE CASE: Someone is kidnapping canines, and it's got the dog-crazy denizens of Fremont all riled up!

THE DETECTIVE: Twelve-year-old Hannah West: aspiring artist, amateur dog-walker, and budding sleuth. At first, Hannah's in heaven in dog-filled Fremont, but when her dog-walking business marks her as a suspect in a series of local dognappings, she knows that this is one case that she's GOT to get to the bottom of—for her own sake, as well as for the sake of her canine companions!